GCSE

Questions and Answers

Q&A

BUSINESS STUDIES

David Floyd: Chief Examiner

Letts

EDUCATIONAL

SERIES EDITOR: BOB McDUELL

Contents

HOW TO USE THIS BOOK

The aim of the *Questions and Answers* series is to provide you with the help required to do as well as possible in your exams at GCSE or, in Scotland, at General and Credit levels. This book is based on the idea that an experienced examiner can give, through examination questions, sample answers and advice, the help students need to secure success and improve their grades.

This *Questions and Answers* series is designed to provide the following.

- **Introductory advice** on the different types of questions and how to answer them to maximise your marks.

- Information about the other skills, apart from the recall of knowledge, that will be tested on examination papers. These are sometimes called **Assessment objectives** and include communication, problem solving, evaluation and interpretation (see pages 3–4). The series develops these skills by showing you how marks are allocated.

- **Revision summaries** to remind you of the topics you will need to have revised in order to answer examination questions.

- Many examples of **examination questions**, arranged by topic, with spaces for you to fill in your answers, just as on an examination paper. Only try the questions once you have revised a topic thoroughly. Read the Revision summary before attempting the questions to double-check you know the topic. It is best not to consult the answers before trying the questions.

- **Sample answers** to all of the questions.

- **Advice from examiners**. By drawing on the experience of actual Chief Examiners we are able to give advice on how you can improve your answers and avoid the most common mistakes.

THE IMPORTANCE OF USING QUESTIONS FOR REVISION

Past examination questions play an important part in revising for examinations. However, it is important not to start practising questions too early. Nothing can be more disheartening than trying to do a question which you do not understand because you have not mastered the topic. Therefore, it is important to have studied a topic thoroughly before attempting any questions on it.

How can past examination questions provide a way of preparing for the examination? It is unlikely that any question you try will appear in exactly the same form on the papers you are going to take. However, the examiner is restricted on what can be set because the questions must cover the whole syllabus and test certain Assessment objectives. The number of totally original questions that can be set on any part of the syllabus is very limited and so similar ideas occur over and over again. Certainly, it will help you if the question you are trying to answer in an examination is familiar, and if you know you have done similar questions before. This is a great boost for your confidence, and confidence is what is required for examination success.

Practising examination questions will also highlight gaps in your knowledge and understanding which you can go back and revise more thoroughly. It will also indicate which sorts of questions you can do well and which, if there is a choice of questions, you should avoid.

Attempting past questions will get you used to the type of language used in questions.

Finally, having access to answers, as you do in this book, will enable you to see clearly what is required by the examiner, how best to answer each question, and the amount of detail required. Attention to detail is a key aspect of achieving success at GCSE.

EXAMINATION TECHNIQUE

One of the keys to examination success is to know how marks are gained and lost by candidates. There are two important aspects to this: ensuring you follow the instructions (or 'rubric') on the examination paper and understanding how examination papers are marked by examiners.

Often candidates do not follow the rubric exactly. If you are asked to answer four questions from a section and you answer five, you can only receive credit for four. The examiner may be instructed to mark the first four only and cross out additional answers. It would be unfortunate if the fifth answer was your best. Anyway, attempting too many questions means you will have wasted time and your answers could have suffered as a result.

Where a choice of questions is possible, candidates often choose the wrong questions. A question which looks familiar may not always be as easy as it seems. If you have a choice, spend time reading all of the questions and making rough notes before you start. Then begin with the questions you think you can do the best and leave any you are not sure about until later. When choosing, look at the marks allocated to various parts of the questions and try to judge if you are confident in those parts where most marks are available.

For every examination paper there is a mark scheme, which tells the examiner where marks should and should not be awarded. For example, where a question is worth a maximum of five marks, there will be five, six or maybe more correct marking points and the examiner will award the first five given by the candidate. A '(5)' shown after a question on an exam paper is an indication that five relevant points are required from your answer. Look at your answers critically after you have written them and try to decide how many different important points you have made.

It is important to read and study carefully the data – the stimulus material – given in the question. One of the main weaknesses shown by GCSE Business Studies candidates is an inability to use the information given in the question. Don't be prepared to write a series of general points, simply because you can remember them. The question will probably require you to relate general points to the particular situation being described. Only by reading and studying the information given, and applying your knowledge to that information, can you obtain most or all of the marks.

You must also remember that you can gain an extra 5% for SPG: Spelling, Punctuation and Grammar. The quality of your answer depends to a large extent on your ability to use business studies terms and language in an appropriate way. These technical words and terms must be spelt correctly and used accurately to gain most or all of the marks available for SPG. If you have time left at the end of the examination, do check carefully what you have written. Have you:

● used complete sentences where necessary;
● spelt words correctly (especially business studies words and terms);
● used correct punctuation and grammar?

Finally, you must manage the time available as effectively as you can. Divide the examination time sensibly between the questions to make sure that you do not spend too long on any one question. When examiners mark the papers of candidates who spend too much time on one question, they often find the candidates have lost far more marks through missing out points in their other answers than they have gained by answering one question in great detail. Many points candidates make in the later stages of an over-long answer turn out to be a repeat of ones made earlier in the answer: there are no marks awarded for repetition.

TYPES OF EXAMINATION QUESTION

The most common types of examination question found in GCSE Business Studies papers are:
● restricted response questions;
● data response questions.

Restricted response questions

These questions usually test your ability to **recall and describe factual business studies content**. They do not normally test your ability to explain an important business concept or idea, or how it relates to a key theme from the syllabus. These questions are sometimes set as **multiple choice** items, where you are required to select the correct answer from three or four alternatives given.

Another common form of restricted response question is the **short-answer** type, which asks you to read a brief question and then write one or two sentences (or possibly only a few words) as the answer. The question might simply test your ability to recall an important fact, or the examiner might link it to data contained in the examination paper; in the latter form these are 'data response' questions. It is important for you to realise that restricted response questions tend to require more limited answers than the full data response ones.

The examiner tends to use key words or phrases such as **state**, **list**, **name**, **outline** or **describe briefly** to indicate that a short answer only is required. Quite often, these questions are set in an examination paper that also doubles as an answer book: the space (number of lines) allowed for your answer indicates the restricted nature of the question. Another obvious clue is that only a few marks are available for a restricted response question.

Data response questions

In studying the world of business, you will have come across many real-life examples and illustrations. Examiners often set questions based on information or 'data' given in the paper. Your task is to answer the questions in the context of the information given: in other words, you respond to the data. There can be an overlap between short-answer and data response questions: most major examination questions are **structured** by being divided into several parts, each requiring only a short answer. There is often an 'incline of difficulty' built into these questions, with the earlier parts of the question being less demanding than the later parts. Structured questions are extremely common in GCSE Business Studies examinations because they are so versatile. The shorter type of structured question is often written for the Foundation papers designed for candidates likely to achieve grade C or below: more demanding structured questions can then be written for the Higher papers (up to and including the A* grade).

Importantly, a data response question requires you to demonstrate two key skills. You must be able to:

- **organise your answer**, and write full sentences and paragraphs
- **link** the general business-related points in your answer to the particular situation given in the data.

ASSESSMENT OBJECTIVES

Assessment objectives are those qualities which are tested in GCSE coursework and examinations. There are four Assessment objectives which are common to all syllabuses in business studies. You will see that only one of these objectives – the first one – concentrates on content knowledge. The others highlight the importance of being able to use this knowledge effectively, and indicate therefore that most of the marks in a GCSE Business Studies examination are not awarded for recalling content knowledge.

Objective 1 *(assessment weighting 25%)*: demonstrating knowledge and critical understanding of specified subject content

This is the Assessment objective which is concerned with your **factual knowledge** of the subject. In any examination, your ability to show that you know and understand the content studied is of great importance. It is possibly the most important ability, because a lack of this background knowledge will mean that you cannot successfully achieve the other objectives. Business studies examinations expect you to show knowledge and understanding of:

- the relationship between business activity and the environment within which it takes place;
- the structure, organisation and control of the main forms of business.

The 'demonstrate knowledge' section of this Assessment objective is often tested within the other objectives. On its own, it is rather limited and GCSE questions based on it are often only multiple choice or short-answer ones. The 'critical understanding' element goes further, in that it tests your ability to **analyse** and **construct explanations** from business studies. It is not sufficient to write down information memorised for the examination, because you also need to show that you understand these concepts. When tackling any of these questions, therefore, you must check that your answer contains a clear and relevant explanation of the business term or concept being tested.

Objective 2 *(assessment weighting 25%)*: applying the specified terms, concepts, theories and methods effectively to address problems and issues

This Assessment objective requires you to apply your content knowledge to the following areas of business activity:

- aims and objectives of a business;
- how a business judges its success;
- roles and relationships existing in business;
- how finance is obtained and managed;
- production and marketing activities.

To answer questions based on this Assessment objective, you have to **relate your content knowledge to the situation described** in the examination paper. For example, an examination might contain information about a firm's financial situation with a question asking you to calculate ratios or suggest a suitable source of finance. Another example could involve you being given details about a company and a proposed new product, then being asked to identify suitable advertising and marketing policies. Here, you are applying your knowledge of marketing to the problem of launching a new product.

Objective 3 *(assessment weighting 25%)*: selecting, organising, interpreting and using information from various sources

In questions testing this Assessment objective you have to show that you can use business studies information which is in **text and/or pictorial format**. For example, you are often asked to select information from a chart or table and then use it in another form. You might have to draw a new graph or chart, or be asked to change text information into diagrams or vice versa. You may also be required to finish a part-completed table or graph, normally on a Foundation level paper. For a Higher level paper you are more likely to be given blank graph paper and asked to select your own scale, for example when constructing a break-even chart.

Objective 4 *(assessment weighting 25%)*: evaluating evidence, making reasoned judgements and presenting conclusions accurately and appropriately

To answer questions based on this Assessment objective you have to be able to **reach a conclusion** about the problem or issue on which you have been tested. The evidence on which you make a judgement is normally presented in the data. Your task is to balance the arguments and use relevant business studies approaches to quantify or 'translate' the evidence. For example, you might judge the financial information mentioned in Objective 2 by using the results of your ratio analysis to reach a conclusion about the firm's profitability and liquidity (its financial stability).

This objective not only tests your ability to reach a sensible conclusion, it also requires you to present your findings 'accurately and appropriately'. Therefore, you will need to identify alternative ways of presenting information, and choose an appropriate one.

Organisations in the economy are classified according to what they produce or provide.

- **Primary:** extractive industries such as the '3 Fs' (farming, fishing and forestry).
- **Secondary**: organisations that manufacture products or construct roads, buildings, etc.
- **Tertiary:** organisations providing services – either commercial services (e.g. banking, transport and insurance) or direct community services (e.g. the emergency services).

Another way of classifying organisations results from the UK's **mixed economy**. The 'mix' consists of the private sector and the public sector. **Private sector** firms are owned by individuals who hope to make a profit. The **public sector** consists of national and local government organisations, where the emphasis is less on the profit motive and more on providing a service for the community.

Firms use resources, known as factors of production. The four factors are **land**, **capital**, **labour** and **enterprise**. The first three factors are combined and used by entrepreneurs (the enterprise factor of production) in producing their goods and services. They set up private sector organisations in the hope of making profits, and as business owners and decision-takers, they bear the risk of making a loss. Entrepreneurs try to combine and use the other factors of production in the most efficient way. The **price mechanism** helps them make decisions. Entrepreneurs compare the relative prices (or costs) of each factor of production and, where possible, substitute a cheaper factor for a more expensive one.

Specialisation helps entrepreneurs, their businesses and advanced economies generally, to function more efficiently. This greater efficiency comes through the use of specialist tools and equipment, and by people developing specialised skills. Countries also tend to specialize in products or services, such as the UK specialising in certain manufactured goods. As a result of specialising, however, a country cannot produce everything it needs for its population. It must therefore **trade** with other countries by importing and exporting, selling the surpluses that result from specialisation: countries become **interdependent**.

People also specialise and become dependent upon others. They require a **medium of exchange** to buy what they need. Money serves this function. It also functions as a **measure of value**, as it allows us to establish a price for something, and as a **store of value** – it can be saved. Savings can be invested by the saver or a borrower with a view to making profit. To encourage savings to take place, interest is paid on them.

Through specialisation, people develop particular skills. Problems of unemployment (and the need to retrain) arise if these skills become obsolete. Specialists who are in employment, whilst helping their organisations operate efficiently, may face problems such as the boredom which can come from doing repetitive tasks. Where tasks are repetitive, there is scope to replace people (the labour factor of production) with machines (the capital factor of production). This leads to higher labour unemployment, which in turn leads to higher social and other costs.

If you need to revise this subject more thoroughly, see the relevant topics in the *Letts* GCSE *Business Studies Study Guide*.

One of the key decisions an entrepreneur must make is **where to locate the business**. Location is influenced by one or more of the following:

- where other firms in the same industry are based (possible **external economies**)
- the proximity, and ease of access, to the firm's:
  - **suppliers**,
  - **markets**;
- the availability of:
  - suitably skilled **labour**,
  - a suitable **site**,
  - UK government, European Union or other **finance** towards the cost,
  - suitable infrastructure (road, rail, air or sea);
- the **personal choice** of the owners/decision-makers.

1 Jane works in the Personnel Department of a large company. Other specialist departments include Sales, Accounts and Buying. Explain **one** advantage and **one** disadvantage to a company from having employees who specialise in one business function only.

Advantage: ....

.... (2)

Disadvantage: ....

.... (2)

2 Which **two** of the following are examples of *invisible exports*?

Holidays taken by British tourists in Spain; British-made cars sold in America; holidays taken by French tourists in Wales; a Japanese company building a factory in Wales; German-made cars sold in Britain; a South American ship insured with Lloyds of London.

(i) ....

(ii) .... (2)

WJEC 1997

3 Which **two** factors will a chain of garages be most likely to take into account in deciding **where** to locate a new garage?
NB *Do not tick more than **two** boxes.*

The number of families with televisions.		The introduction of a new tax on car repairs.	
The amount of competition in the area.		Their spending on a national advertising campaign.	
The increase in demand for new cars throughout the country.		Expected numbers of customers.	

(2)
WJEC 1998

4 Underline the words in italics which are correct in the following sentences.

(a) Marks and Spencer plc is a *public limited company/private limited company* based in the *public sector/private sector*. (2)

(b) Moving to a new site is called *redundancy/relocation/recruitment*. (1)

5 Cannit Ltd makes tins and cans used for storing liquids. These are sold to organisations in both the public and private sectors. Some of Cannit Ltd's products are bought by local authorities. Cannit Ltd sells its products to organisations located in the UK and continental Europe. The company is currently based in the north of England. The directors of Cannit Ltd are considering whether they should relocate the company in either the Midlands or the south-east of England. They are examining sites in two towns:

Town	**Telford**	**Dover**
Location	West Midlands	South-East
Approximate population	150 000	50 000
Local unemployment levels	High	Low
Local living costs	Low	High
Local workforce	Experienced in manufacture	Limited experience in manufacturing industries
Factory units	Widely available: average rent £220 per week	Limited availability: average rent £350 per week
Transport links	Good road and rail links	Good road, rail and sea links, and close to Channel Tunnel
Suppliers	None nearby	Major suppliers nearby

(a) In which sector of production – primary, secondary or tertiary – are the following?

Cannit Ltd: ....

local authorities: .... (2)

(b) In which sector of the economy – private or public – are the following based?

Cannit Ltd: ....

local authorities: .... (2)

(c) Explain **four** factors that Cannit Ltd's directors will consider when taking the decision to relocate.

....

....

....

....

....

....

....

....

.... (12)

(d) Explain **three** business problems the directors of Cannit Ltd might face if they decide to relocate to either Telford or Dover.

....

....

....

....

....

....

....

....

....

.... (6)

(e) Identify **two** business reasons for each town that might encourage the directors to relocate in:

Telford: ....

....

....

.... (2)

Dover: ....

....

....

.... (2)

Organisations in the UK economy can be classified according to their choice of legal structure, the sector in which they operate and their business objectives.

Two key concepts associated with private sector firms are **profit** and **limited liability**. The fact that an organisation is in the private sector normally means it will seek to make at least an acceptable level of profits for its owners. The owners are entrepreneurs with a profit motive, profit being the reward for the **risk** of being in business. Other reasons that people set up private sector firms include:

- the desire for job satisfaction;
- personal goals and reasons;
- the wish for a satisfactory level of income;
- a desire to work.

Limited liability is associated with limited companies: business organisations which must include 'limited' (Ltd) or 'PLC' in their names. Limited liability brings benefits not only to the owners of the company, but also to the economy. It encourages people to set up in business because they realise that there are limits to the amount they can lose if their business venture fails to succeed.

The main forms of private sector business ownership are sole traders, partnerships and limited liability companies. Their business objectives include survival, making a profit and increasing market share. Sole traders and partnerships are two forms of **unincorporated business**. Unlike limited companies, they do not have a separate legal existence from their owners. A **sole trader** business is the easiest and least expensive to establish, and is found where large-scale production is not required. Local service firms such as hairdressing and plumbing are therefore often sole traders. Benefits include independence as well as the ease of setting up, but drawbacks include long working hours, limited specialist knowledge and unlimited liability. **Partnerships** are associated with professions such as dentists and accountants, and have similar advantages and disadvantages to sole traders. Compared with them, partnerships tend to be larger with access to more capital (there are at least two owners), although difficulties arise if one of the partners dies or decides to leave.

There are two categories of limited company, both receiving the benefits of incorporation and limited liability. The **private limited company** cannot advertise its shares for sale to the public or through the Stock Exchange: the owners can keep the affairs of the company more private, and are protected from hostile takeover bids. A **public limited company** (PLC) gains the financial benefit of approaching the public to invest, and its large size often leads to economies of scale. Setting up a PLC, however, is expensive and its large size works against it when diseconomies of scale are found.

Important recent developments in the UK economy include the growth in **franchising** as a form of business ownership.

- The **franchisor** company allows the franchisee to sell its product or service, and supplies equipment and advice. Therefore, the franchisor can expand without the need for major capital investment.

- In return for this, the **franchisee** invests the capital and pays royalties to the franchisor out of profits made, and receives a well-known or well-supported product or service.

The **public sector** provides goods and services typically through either public corporations or local authorities. The profit motive is not so important, although the organisations may have to meet certain financial targets. **Privatisation** has been an important trend here: public corporations have been sold to the private sector in an attempt to bring about the benefits associated with greater competition. The government has received the revenue from privatisation. In many cases, however, a privatised monopoly has been created from the public sector monopoly, and increased competition has not always resulted.

If you need to revise this subject more thoroughly, see the relevant topics in the *Letts* GCSE Business Studies Study Guide.

1 Which **three** of the following statements apply to public limited companies?
   NB *Do not tick more than* **three** *boxes*.

The name of the company is followed by the letters 'plc'.		The name of the company is followed by the letters 'Ltd'.	
The maximum number of shareholders is twenty.		Shares are sold on the Stock Exchange.	
Shares cannot be sold to members of the general public.		They have a maximum share capital of £50000.	
They are owned by the government on behalf of the people.		They have limited liability.	

(3)

WJEC 1998

2 The following features are associated with either a sole trader, a partnership, or one or other of the types of limited company. Identify *the most appropriate form* of business ownership for each feature by ticking the relevant box.

	Sole trader	Part-nership	Ltd co.	PLC
(a) One person is in complete control.				
(b) Shares are sold to the public at large.				
(c) There are typically between two and 20 owners.				
(d) All profits go to the owner, who also has to bear all the losses.				
(e) Shares are issued but not sold to the general public.				
(f) The organisation starts trading when it receives its Certificate of Incorporation.				
(g) The owners normally draw up a written agreement.				
(h) Economies of scale are easiest to achieve.				

(8)

3 Oakwell Ltd is based in Bristol. Its main activity is making high-quality wooden furniture. It was originally set up as a partnership by its two owners. After taking advice, they changed the status of the firm to a private limited company. The company has grown dramatically in the last five years. One of the owners wants to change the company's status to that of a PLC.

(a) Suggest **two** reasons why it might be better for the owners to operate Oakwell as a private limited company rather than as a partnership.

QUESTIONS

....

....

....

.... (4)

(b) In what way is the term *limited* in Oakwell's name a warning to those who trade with it?

....

.... (2)

(c) What is meant by the term *PLC*?

....

.... (2)

(d) Why might the other owner wish to keep Oakwell as a private limited company?

....

.... (2)

(e) What will Oakwell Ltd's Memorandum and Articles of Association contain?

Memorandum: ....

.... (2)

Articles: ....

.... (2)

(f) Assume Oakwell becomes a PLC. Explain **two** ways in which the ownership and control of a PLC such as Oakwell differs from that of a public corporation.

....

....

.... (4)

4 The UK has seen many privatised monopolies develop during the 1980s and 1990s. Examples include National Power plc and BT plc.

(a) Explain how a monopoly differs from firms in a more competitive market.

....

.... (2)

(b) Why does the government seek to control monopolies?

....

.... (2)

(c) Identify and explain **one** way in which monopolies can operate to the consumer's benefit.

....

.... (2)

(d) Explain the meaning of the term *privatisation*.

.... (2)

(e) Give **one** argument for, and **one** argument against, privatising state-owned industries.

For: ....

....

Against: ....

.... (4)

(f) Explain **one** benefit of privatisation for:

(i) the government: ....

....

(ii) the firms involved: ....

....

(iii) consumers: ....

.... (3)

5 In May 1996 Hash Patel was made redundant. He decided to buy his own 'corner shop' selling newspapers and magazines, confectionery and tobacco.

(a) What is likely to have motivated Hash to buy and run his own business?

....

.... (2)

Hash has now sold his shop and taken out a franchise with a major UK petrol supplier. He runs a garage selling the company's petrol, as well as the garage shop.

(b) What is the name given to:

(i) a person such as Hash who invests in a franchise? ....

(ii) the company granting the franchise? .... (2)

(c) Describe **two** advantages and **two** disadvantages to Hash from taking out a franchise rather than setting up in business as a completely independent sole trader.

....

....

....

.... (4)

(d) (i) State **two** business objectives that Hash will now have.

....

.... (2)

(ii) Contrast the business objectives of Hash with those of the company from which he is franchising.

....

....

....

.... (4)

3 Business finance and growth

The size of a firm can be measured in different ways. Popular bases are:

- **profit**;
- **turnover**;
- **number of employees**;
- **capital employed**;
- **market share**.

Firms grow through internal or **organic** growth. This expansion is achieved through extra finance and reinvesting (ploughing back) profits, with the firm expanding its product range or moving into new markets. It is a slow process, so many firms seek to grow more quickly through merger or takeover. **Mergers** take place between two firms agreeing to join together. **Takeovers** occur when one company purchases sufficient voting shares in another company to give it control of that company.

Firms are able to grow more quickly as a result of mergers and/or takeovers. The **integration** that takes place as a result of the new company reorganising its activities can be as follows.

- **Horizontal**: this occurs when firms in the **same industry** and at the **same stage of production** (primary, secondary or tertiary) combine – for example, two vehicle manufacturers may merge production. Larger-scale production and economies of scale should result from this integration.

- **Vertical**: this occurs between firms in the same industry but at **different stages of production** – an example is a brewery (secondary) taking over a public house (tertiary). Advantages include greater control of supply (if integration is 'backwards') and better access to the market (if 'forwards').

- **Lateral** also known as **conglomerate** integration: this occurs when a company moves into a new product area or market as a result of the merger/takeover. This leads to greater **diversification**, which reduces the risk for the company: it is now not as dependent on one market or one product.

Growth requires **financing**. In the public sector, the major sources of finance for a public corporation are from its own trading activities, general taxation and borrowing from the Treasury. In the private sector, there are many different sources of finance available to firms. These can be either **short term** or **long term**, and can arise from **internal** sources or be obtained from **external** sources.

The key internal source of finance is **retained profits**. Owners must make a choice: do they spend net profit by withdrawing it out of the firm (including issuing it as dividends), or do they keep it in the firm (more cash is kept in the firm which helps expansion)?

The main external long-term source of finance is **capital invested**. Sole traders and partners find their own capital, for example from personal savings. Companies issue shares, the two main types being as follows.

- **Ordinary**: 'equity' capital, giving a vote at the Annual General Meeting (AGM), with the shareholder receiving a variable rate of dividend after all other dividends and payments have been made out of profits.

- **Preference**: the shareholder receives a fixed dividend after debenture interest and other deductions are made, but before the ordinary dividend is declared – these are less of a gamble than ordinary shares, but the owner does not have a vote.

A company may also obtain long-term loan capital by issuing **debentures**. These long-term loans receive interest which must be paid (whereas a dividend does not have to be paid). Debenture holders are not owners of the company in the same way that shareholders are.

In addition to share and loan capital, the major external sources of finance include:

❶ **trade credit**: taking advantage of the credit period allowed by suppliers;

❷ **factoring**: the firm sells its debts for less than their face value to a factoring company, receiving immediate cash;

❸ **bank overdrafts**: based on a current account, the owner(s) can overdraw up to an agreed maximum figure;

❹ **bank and other loans**: longer term than overdrafts, for a fixed amount and for a fixed period;

❺ **leasing**: the firm agrees with a finance house to lease capital equipment, to avoid the cost of buying it; **hire purchase** and **credit sale** agreements can also be used by the firm to finance the purchase of fixed assets.

Finance is vital to a firm, both for growth and for **survival**. The owners will forecast their **cash-flows** to see whether they can meet their debts out of cash inflows, or whether they need to make arrangements to borrow money. Companies are now obliged to produce a cash-flow analysis as part of their published accounts. A cash flow statement can be organised as follows.

	January £000	February £000	March £000
RECEIPTS			
Sales	20	18	20
Other receipts	2	–	–
Total receipts	22	18	20
PAYMENTS			
Materials	6	5	6
Wages	8	8	8
Other expenses	2	2	2
Capital expenditure	–	10	–
Total payments	16	25	16
Net cash surplus or deficit	6	(7)	4
Cash balance from last month	40	46	39
Cash balance carried forward to next month	46	39	43

If you need to revise this subject more thoroughly, see the relevant topics in the *Letts* GCSE *Business Studies Study Guide.*

1 Identify and explain the importance of **three** factors that help determine the sources of finance used by the owners of firms.

....

....

....

....

....

.... (6)

2 Which of the following is an example of *horizontal* integration?

(a) A clothing manufacturer merging with a high-street chain of clothing shops.

(b) A chemical company taking over a food manufacturer.

(c) Two film companies merging.

(d) A chemical company buying a chain of chemist shops.

Answer .... (1)

3 Explain briefly how a change in interest rates affects a firm's profitability.

....

.... (2)

4 Alan and Raj are partners who have established a small manufacturing business. They now need to buy raw materials and a machine to start production. To finance the purchase of materials, Alan has arranged a bank overdraft, and Raj is negotiating a bank loan to buy the machine.

(a) Explain why each method of finance is appropriate in this situation.

Overdraft: ....

....

Loan: ....

....

.... (4)

(b) Identify **one** alternative method of finance for the materials and **one** alternative for the machine. In each case:

(i) explain why it is a suitable alternative method;

(ii) describe one disadvantage it has as a method of finance.

Alternative to overdraft: ....

....

Disadvantage: ....

....

Alternative to bank loan: ....

....

Disadvantage: ....

.... (6)

5   Joan used to work for a *multinational* conglomerate which originally concentrated on refining oil. This *conglomerate* took over another oil refining company several years ago, and it also now owns several petrol station chains throughout Europe as well as hotels and entertainment complexes.
Joan has set up in business for herself, and has bought a large old property by the sea in order to run a guest house. She has now decided to *diversify* by opening up her front rooms as a coffee shop, but she needs to find:
*   £8000 for the cost of alterations to the building;
*   £1500 for furniture, coffee- and tea-making equipment and a refrigerator;
*   £500 for initial stock.

(a) From the above information:

(i) Explain the terms in italics.

Multinational: ....

Conglomerate: ....

Diversify: .... (3)

(ii) Identify the evidence which suggests that the following integration has taken place:

1. Horizontal: ....

....

2. Vertical: ....

....

3. Lateral: ....

.... (3)

(b) What form of business ownership is a multinational likely to be?

.... (1)

(c) Explain how vertical integration can make a company more competitive.

....

....

....

.... (2)

(d) Identify **one** appropriate source of finance for each of the amounts Joan needs to find. State why each source is appropriate.

£8000: ....

....

£1500: ....

....

£500: .... (6)

6   **Carolian Leather Goods**
Ten years ago Ian Garner set up his own business producing leather and stationery items.
This included leather-bound personal organisers, ring binders and photograph frames.
Before being make redundant, Ian had 15 years experience working for a large company
producing similar goods but with a larger product range. Ian used his redundancy money and
all his savings to set the business up.
The first years were not easy, Ian worked very long hours to get the business going. Carol,
his wife, was worried about the risks of Ian setting up his own business. To begin with, Ian
was the only person who had the skills needed for the production of the goods. Carol helped
with the administration of the business. The last five years have been easier, Ian has been
able to employ more staff and concentrate on increasing sales turnover. He has widened the
product range and increased the number of outlets selling his goods.

(a) Explain why Ian might have considered setting up his own business.

....

....

....

....

....

....

....

.... (5)

(b) (i)   Describe the objectives the business may have had in the early years.

....

....

....

....

....

....

.... (6)

(ii) Explain how the business objectives of Carolian might change over time.

....

....

QUESTIONS

....

....

....

....

....

....

.... (8)

(c) Explain the risks for Ian in running his own business.

....

....

....

....

....

....

.... (6)

(d) Ian was fortunate that the redundancy money and his savings were enough to start the business. Describe other sources of finance he could have tried to obtain and explain which method you think would have been best.

....

....

....

....

....

....

....

....

....

.... (12)

NEAB 1997

One important way to classify production costs is to divide them into fixed and variable. **Fixed costs** do not change as output changes: examples include factory rent and office workers' salaries. **Variable costs** do change as output changes: examples include the cost of raw materials to make the product and 'piecework' wages. In practice, many costs are **semi-variable**, having both a fixed and a variable element. An example is the cost of power such as electricity; this often has a standing charge payable whether any power is used or not, and on top of this users pay per unit of electricity used.

This distinction is important to business people because it helps them **make decisions**. One common application is **break-even analysis**. A product's unit **contribution** – the difference between its selling price and its variable cost – can be calculated. Each unit contribution goes towards the firm's fixed costs, which must be paid whether or not anything is made. It is now possible to calculate the product's break-even point, which is the number of units that must be made and sold to cover total fixed costs.

$$\textbf{Break-even point} = \frac{\text{Total fixed costs}}{\text{Unit contribution}}$$

Another way to explain the break-even point is as the point at which the firm makes **neither a profit nor a loss**. This gives owners information about the sales they must make to cover their costs, and the product's margin of safety, i.e. the difference between the number the owners expect to sell and the number they need to sell to break even.

The way that firms are organised to make their products varies. There are three main manufacturing (or production) methods:

- **job** production: making 'one-off' items (a single, unique product), such as building an individually designed office block or a 'made-to-measure' item of clothing;

- **batch** production: a set number of the same product is made, before production switches to a batch of a different product – examples include books and certain items of furniture;

- **mass** (also known as process or flow) production: large numbers of an identical product are made, and so this form of production is associated with mass-market items, such as cars, televisions and other consumer durables.

The way production is organised influences the factory layout, the skills needed by employees and how capital-intensive or labour-intensive production will be. Job production typically requires skilled labour, whereas mass production often involves a more capital-intensive approach to manufacture.

Mass production is the form most closely associated with **economies of scale**. One effect of a firm growing in size and using modern production techniques is that its increased output is spread over the same total fixed costs. Greater production means greater total costs, but economies of scale result in the firm having **lower unit costs** as output levels rise. The main economies of scale include:

- **financial**: increased size makes borrowing easier and less costly;

- **managerial**: efficient specialists can be employed who bring greater expertise into the firm;

- **marketing**: specialist marketing agencies can be employed, and marketing costs can be spread over a large output, reducing their unit costs;

- **purchasing**: bulk buying discounts become possible;

- **technological**: larger firms are better able to support research and development, and will benefit from any technological developments that result;

- **increased dimensions**: doubling the size of something does not usually double its cost – for example, large firms can buy large-scale transport which is less expensive per item transported.

If you need to revise this subject more thoroughly, see the relevant topics in the *Letts* GCSE *Business Studies Study Guide*.

1 The **job** method of production is associated with making:

(a) cars

(b) ships

(c) computers

(d) books.

Answer:.......................... (1)

2 Which **three** of the following are examples of *fixed costs*?
NB *Do not tick more than* **three** *boxes*.

Payment for machinery.		Bill for electricity to power machines.	
Cost of packaging.		Raw materials.	
Value Added Tax.		Rates.	
Cost of buying vans.		Petrol for delivery vehicles.	

(3)

WJEC 1998

3 A company's normal output is 500 units: its production costs total £3400. The accountant has calculated that if the company made 510 units, costs would rise to £3550. Calculate:

(a) the variable cost for each of the 10 extra units:

....

.... (2)

(b) the company's average cost of production for 500 units:

....

.... (2)

4 The following table shows the range of possible production for the 'Sucker' vacuum cleaner made at one factory owned by Suckit Ltd, a company making a range of vacuum cleaners.

Expected yearly sales (000)	Cost price (£)	Selling price (£)
10	65	80
20	55	70
30	50	65
40	55	65

(a) The company uses batch production at this factory. Explain this method of production.

....

.... (2)

(b) Suggest **one** reason why the directors do not use the mass (or flow) method of production.

....

.... (2)

(c) Use the information in the table to show how Suckit Ltd gains from economies of scale.

....

....

....

.... (4)

(d) Identify and explain **two** economies of scale from which this company might benefit.

(i) ....

....

(ii) ....

.... (4)

(e) The directors have decided to make and sell 30 000 'Sucker' cleaners. Explain why they have decided not to make and sell 40 000 units a year.

....

....

....

.... (4)

5 (a) Louisa uses break-even analysis to calculate how many dresses must be made before the business makes a profit. The selling price of a dress is £700.
A part-completed table is shown below.

LOUISA DESIGNS: COSTS AND REVENUE

No. of dresses	0	50	100	150	200	250
Fixed costs (£)	75 000	75 000	75 000	75 000	75 000	75 000
Variable costs (£)	0	15 000	30 000	45 000	60 000	75 000
Total costs (£)	75 000	90 000	105 000	120 000	135 000	150 000
Revenue (£)						

(i)   On the table above, complete the blank spaces to show the revenue.   (1)
(ii) On the partly-completed break-even chart below:
      • plot the revenue line;
      • label the other two lines.   (3)
(iii) Label the break-even output.   (1)
(iv) From the chart, estimate how many dresses Louisa will have to sell to break even.

....   (1)

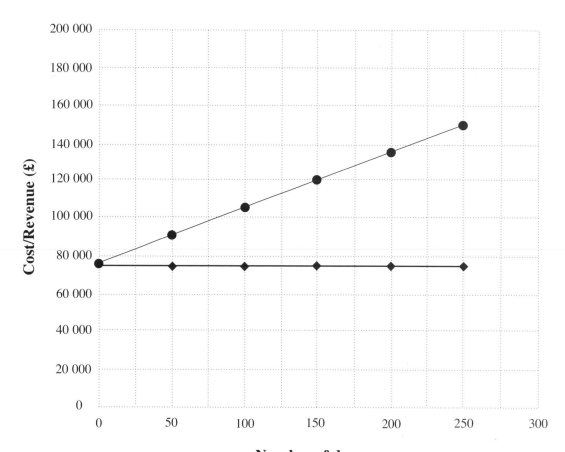

(b) (i) Explain what is meant by fixed costs and give **ONE** example.

....

.... (2)

(ii) Explain what is meant by variable costs and give **ONE** example.

....

.... (2)

(c) (i) At present *Louisa Designs* uses job production. Explain what this is.

....

.... (2)

(ii) Explain the difference between batch and flow production.

....

....

.... (4)

(iii) Explain the possible effects on employees if *Louisa Designs* moves from job to batch or flow production.

....

....

.... (4)

Edexcel 1996

6 Alan Fredericks has established his own photography business. He works in a studio and pays £100 rent per month. Alan employs a part-time assistant at a monthly salary of £200. He calculates that each photograph will cost him 20p for the film, 30p to develop and 50p for its frame. He expects to sell 2000 photographs in the first year, at a price of £6.00 each.

(a) Calculate how many photographs Alan must sell in his first year in order to break even.

....

.... (2)

(b) Construct Alan's break-even chart for his first year using the graph on the next page.

(5)

(c) Use your break-even chart to identify:

(i) Alan's break-even number of sales: ....

(ii) his break-even revenue: ....

(iii) the profit Alan expects to make in his first year: ....

(iv) the profit or loss if he only sells 1000 photos: ....

(v) his margin of safety if he sells 2000 photos: .... (5)

(d) Alan believes he could sell 2500 photographs if he reduced the price of each photograph to £5. Explain whether Alan should drop his price. Support your answer with relevant calculations or illustrations.

....

....

....

....

....

....

.... (10)

The role of a private sector firm's accounting function is to **record**, **present** and **analyse** financial information. This information is recorded in accounts which are grouped into ledgers:

- the **Sales Ledger** contains the accounts of debtors (customers buying on credit);
- the **Purchases Ledger** holds the accounts of creditors (suppliers of goods on credit);
- the **Cash Book** contains records of cash and bank transactions;
- the **Nominal** (or **General**) **Ledger** stores the other accounts.

These accounts are then presented and summarised in the firm's final accounts.

	Profit and Loss account	**Balance Sheet**
Purpose:	To calculate net profit	To show the firm's financial position
Contents:	Revenues (income) and expenses: **revenue expenditure**	Assets (items owned by the firm) and Liabilities (items owed by the firm): **capital expenditure**

Accountants also produce **cash flow statements** which analyse the movements in the cash and bank balances and summarise the firm's liquidity, that is its ability to meet its debts as they fall due.

Accounting ratios are used to analyse financial information. Two major **profitability** ratios are:

$$\textbf{ROCE (return on capital employed)} = \frac{\text{Net Profit x 100}}{\text{Capital employed}}$$

This shows the rate of return on capital, and can be compared with the rate an investor could receive elsewhere, for example by investing in a safer fixed-interest source such as a building society account.

$$\textbf{Net Profit Margin} = \frac{\text{Net Profit x 100}}{\text{Sales}}$$

This shows how many pence in each £'s worth of sales is represented by net profit. This gives information on whether the selling price could be dropped (by cutting this margin) in an attempt to increase sales.

The main **liquidity** ratio is the Current Ratio:

$$\textbf{Current Ratio} = \text{Current Assets: Current Liabilities}$$

A ratio of 2:1 tells us that there is £2 cash or 'near-cash' available to pay short-term debts. The difference between the current assets (stock, debtors and cash) and current liabilities (creditors and bank overdraft) is called **Working Capital**. In practice, many large firms, especially in the retail sector, have a negative working capital, a ratio less than 1:1, but still survive financially.

Accountants also remove stock from the Current Assets total to calculate the Liquid Assets (also known as the Acid Test) ratio. This informs them whether the firm's cash and debtor resources are sufficient to meet its own short-term debts, without having to sell any stock.

Efficiency ratios are also used by accountants. These include 'debtor days' and 'creditor days' which show how many days' credit the firm allows and takes respectively. This is important information for credit control purposes.

$$\textbf{Debtor Days} = \frac{\text{Debtors x 365}}{\text{Sales}} \qquad \textbf{Creditor Days} = \frac{\text{Creditors x 365}}{\text{Sales}}$$

Another efficiency ratio is the Rate of Stock Turnover ('Stockturn') which calculates the number of times the firm's average stock is sold or 'turned over' during the period.

$$\textbf{Rate of Stock Turnover} = \frac{\text{Cost of sales}}{\text{Average stock}}$$

1 A company's Trading and Profit and Loss account includes the following information:

Sales	Cost of Sales	Gross Profit	Net Profit
£300 000	£225 000	£75 000	£30 000

Calculate the firm's Gross Profit Margin and Net Profit Margin. Show your workings.

Gross Profit Margin:

....

....

....

....

Net Profit Margin:

....

....

....

.... (4)

2 For each of the following items place a tick in the appropriate column to indicate whether it is an example of revenue expenditure or capital expenditure.

	Revenue expenditure	Capital expenditure
Purchase of new computer system.	....	....
Rental fee paid for new photocopier.	....	....
Sales office staff salaries.	....	....
Cost of new factory extension.	....	....
Purchase of new delivery vehicle.	....	....
Petrol costs for the delivery vehicle.	....	.... (6)

3 (a) Bubbles (UK) Limited is a private company manufacturing leisure wear. Its annual accounts show the company's Gross Profit and Net Profit.

Explain the difference between the Gross Profit and the Net Profit of a business.

1. Gross Profit ....

....

....

2. Net Profit ....

....

.... (4)

(b) Study the Trading Accounts of Bubbles (UK) Ltd shown below and answer the questions which follow.

Trading Accounts for Years ended 31 December

		1993		1994
		£		£
Sales		200 000		250 000
Cost of Sales		120 000	(ii)	[ ]
Gross Profit	(i)	[ ]		100 000

Using the information provided, calculate the figures missing from boxes (i) and (ii). Write your answers in the boxes.

Show your calculation below.

....

....

....

....

.... (4)

(c) Bubbles (UK) Ltd's expenses in 1993 were £50 000. What was the company's Net Profit? Show your working.

....

....

.... (2)

(d) (i) What is meant by a firm's rate of turnover?

....

....

.... (2)

(ii) The stocks of Bubbles UK Ltd were: on 1 January 93   £25 000
                                          on 31 December 93   £15 000

Calculate the company's rate of turnover for 1993. Show your working.

....

....

....

....

....

.... (5)

(iii) The company's sales increased in 1994. State **three** reasons which might explain why this happened.

1...

....

2...

....

3...

.... (3)

(e) Bubbles (UK) Ltd's summarised Balance Sheets are shown below.

Balance Sheets as at 31 December

	1993 £000s	1994 £000s		1993 £000s	1994 £000s
Ordinary Share Capital	120	150	Fixed Assets	150	200
Reserves	30	60	Current Assets	25	30
Current Liabilities	25	20			
	175	230		175	230

(i) State **two** features of Ordinary Shares.

1 ....

....

2 ....

.... (2)

(ii) What change took place in the company's Fixed Assets between 1993 and 1994?

....

....

....

.... (3)

(iii) Describe how the company's **Net** Current Assets changed between 1993 and 1994?

....

....

....

.... (3)

(iv) Name **three** sources of long-term capital which Bubbles (UK) Ltd could use to finance the purchase of new fixed assets.

1..

2..

3.. (3)

(f) (i) Bubbles (UK) Ltd's capital employed has changed between 1993 and 1994.

What is meant by the 'capital employed' in a company?

....

....

.... (2)

(ii) Bubbles (UK) Ltd's Net Profit in 1994 was £40 000.

What was the rate of return on the capital employed in the company in 1994? Show all your workings.

....

....

....

.... (3)

(iii) What is the importance of the return on the capital employed to a shareholder in the company?

....

....

....

....

.... (4)

MEG 1995

All firms depend for their survival on a contented and efficient workforce: its human resource. A firm's **Personnel** function manages its human resources.

In order to recruit suitable staff, the department with the vacancy needs to inform Personnel of:

- the nature of and duties associated with the post – the **job description**;
- the personal qualities required by the successful applicant – the **person specification**.

Staff in Personnel can then design and place suitable job adverts. The firm might **recruit** internally, for example on notice boards or in a staff newsletter. Internal recruitment (promotion) will increase the motivation level of existing employees. There are various sources for external recruitment; for example, Personnel staff may use Job Centres and/or recruitment agencies, or choose to advertise in an appropriate newspaper.

For **selection**, applicants need to be shortlisted. This is achieved by comparing their experience and qualifications – shown on their application forms or curriculum vitae – against the job description and person specification. Interviews are then conducted. These often include selection tests such as aptitude testing. After appointment the Personnel Department will issue the successful applicant with a contract of employment containing information such as hours of work, holidays and holiday pay, and the disciplinary rules.

Once in post, the Personnel Department considers staff **training** needs. The purpose of **induction** training is to familiarise the new member of staff with the firm's activities and structures. Once established, the employee may gain additional skills through **on-the-job** or **off-the-job** training. The former is based 'in-house' with employees learning as they work: training tends to be limited to particular skills and procedures. Off-the-job training involves attending specialist training centres and is more closely associated with obtaining qualifications.

Personnel managers are particularly concerned with ensuring that the firm's employees gain **job satisfaction**. Pay levels are important, although many psychologists suggest that there are several other aspects in making a job satisfying.

Theorist:	Abraham Maslow	Douglas McGregor	Frederick Herzberg
Theory:	A hierarchy of needs require satisfying: once low-level needs such as safety and hunger are satisfied, employees seek to achieve higher-order needs such as social- and self-fulfilment.	A *Theory X* manager assumes people dislike work, and need control and direction. *Theory Y* managers believe their employees want to make positive contributions to the work of the firm.	*Hygiene factors* such as money and working conditions are important, but *motivators* such as achievement and recognition are also needed to motivate employees.

Personnel staff are involved in **negotiation** and **consultation** with trade union representatives. **Trade unions** are employee organisations set up to represent their interests. Popular reasons for joining a trade union are for job protection, to receive members' benefits and to seek higher pay and/or better working conditions. Unions normally aim to:

- protect their members (for example, from unfair dismissal);
- negotiate with employers regarding pay conditions;
- ensure their members receive rights such as maternity benefit to which they are entitled;
- represent their members, for example, at industrial tribunals.

Collective bargaining takes place between employers and trade unions and is a common way to establish pay levels and working conditions. If talks break down and a dispute arises, union members have a number of options available, including holding an official strike. If the dispute continues, employers and unions may resort to **arbitration**, for example, by bringing in **ACAS**, the Advisory Conciliation and Arbitration Service.

If you need to revise this subject more thoroughly, see the relevant topics in the *Letts* GCSE *Business Studies Study Guide.*

1 A *non-financial* incentive for an employee is:

(a) a staff discount scheme

(b) flexitime

(c) subsidised meals

(d) a profit-sharing scheme.

Answer: .... (1)

2 Which **three** of the following are normally the responsibility of a company's *personnel department*? N.B.: *Do not tick more than **three** boxes.*

Interviewing job applicants.		Paying invoices.	
Controlling quality.		Organising transport of finished goods.	
Ordering raw materials.		Planning production.	
Promoting sales.		Training staff.	
Designing new products.		Storage of finished goods.	
Looking after staff welfare.		Carrying out market research.	

(3)

WJEC 1996

3 Osborne Ltd is currently recruiting staff. It has an induction training scheme for all new employees. It also operates 'on-the-job' training and 'off-the-job' training schemes.

(a) (i) Give **two** advantages of recruiting externally, rather than promoting from within.

....

.... (2)

(ii) Name **two** external sources of recruitment the company could use to recruit staff.

....

.... (2)

(b) (i) Identify **three** items likely to be included in Osborne Ltd's induction programme.

1. ....

2. ....

3. .... (3)

(ii) State **one** advantage to the company, and **one** advantage to the employee, from operating an induction training programme.

Osborne Ltd: ....

Employee: .... (2)

(c) (i) Explain the difference between on-the-job training and off-the-job training.

....

.... (2)

(ii) Give **two** reasons why employees may prefer off-the-job training.

....

.... (2)

4 Name **two** Acts of Parliament influencing the contents of a job advertisement.

1. ....   2. .... (2)

5 Below is a job advertisement which Sellit Ltd placed in a local shop window.

> WANTED – SALES PERSONS
>
> Experience desirable/Good wages
>
> Telephone 424906

(a) State **three** other pieces of information that it might be useful to include in the job advertisement.

1. ....

2. ....

3. .... (3)

(b) What problems might arise if the firm employed unsuitable workers?

....

.... (2)

(c) The firm receives very few replies to its advertisement. List **four** reasons which might explain why it received so few replies.

1. ....

2. ....

3. ....

4. .... (4)

(d) Sellit Ltd eventually appoints two new workers to its sales team. The Human Resource manager is asked to draw up an Induction programme for these workers. Why is it advisable for the firm to provide these workers with an Induction programme?

....

....

....

.... (4)

(e) Sellit Ltd pays its sales team a basic salary, plus bonuses when sales targets are reached. Why might the sales team not like this payment system?

....

.... (2)

(f) Apart from changing its payment system, how might Sellit Ltd improve the performance of the sales force?

....

....

....

.... (4)

(g) The main aim of Sellit Ltd is to maximise profits. Describe a situation in which this aim could lead to conflict between management and workers.

....

.... (2)

(h) The issue of whether or not there should be a national minimum wage arises from time to time. What effect do you think the introduction of minimum wage legislation might have on this firm?

....

....

.... (4)

NICCEA 1997

6

Rightway Stores Ltd employs 200 staff in its Welford supermarket. The staff are mainly female and part-time. The store management consists of:

RIGHTWAY STORES LTD

Store Manager
|
Deputy Store Manager

Assistant Manager Personnel | Assistant Manager Check-outs | Assistant Manager Shop floor | Assistant Manager Stock

Rightway has a high turnover of staff. The store manager, Lucy Cliff, feels that this is not really a problem for Rightway Stores.

There are lots of women out there who are keen to work for us. Apart from induction training there are few costs involved in employing new workers.

Lucy Cliff

We employ part-time staff because it is easier to change their hours and they do not get as many benefits as full-time staff.

Ben Crewe
Assistant Manager Personnel

(a) Explain why Rightway employs mainly part-time staff.

....

....

....

....

.... (6)

(b) In spite of what Lucy says, what problems could a high turnover of staff cause Rightway?

....

....

....

....

....

.... (8)

(c) (i) Rightway needs to advertise for part-time staff. Explain, giving reasons, the most effective ways to advertise the vacancies.

....

....

....

....

.... (8)

(ii) Explain what would be the most effective ways for Rightway to select from the applicants for the part-time vacancies.

....

....

....

....

.... (8)

(d) Rightway's induction training lasts for three days. Describe what you would expect to be included in the induction programme.

....

....

....

....

....

....

.... (10)

NEAB 1996

The marketing function has two key roles to play in a firm.

● It collects and analyses data from the firm's markets and from its consumers.

● It promotes and supports the firm's products and services in the marketplace.

Collecting and analysing data involves **market research.** Data are collected by field research and/or desk research. **Field** (also known as primary) research collects original data exclusively for this research purpose. The main technique used to collect data is through completing a **questionnaire** – either through the post, by telephone, or by personal interview. Other techniques include **observing customers** buying products, **test marketing** a product to gain information, and using a **panel of consumers** to comment on products. Although expensive, field research produces information fully relevant to the product being researched. To be effective, field research must use suitable **sampling** techniques because the firm cannot normally obtain information from all its consumers (because of time and cost limitations).

Desk (also known as secondary) research is based on **existing sources** such as the firm's own sales and market data, UK and European official statistical publications, and information from trade associations. Because this information is already available, it is quicker and less expensive to obtain than field research. The main disadvantage of desk research is that it has not been collected specifically for the firm's purpose, and is therefore not always sufficiently detailed or fully relevant.

Markets can be **segmented**: divided into distinct sub-groups. Segmenting a market allows the firm's marketing experts to concentrate their marketing on particular characteristics of either the consumer or the product: these key features of the product or the consumer are used to split markets into their distinct segments. Advertising and other promotion can then focus on certain features of the product, or characteristics of consumers in the segment. Some firms concentrate on making products for small and distinct market segments – **niche markets** – whereas other firms (many multinationals, for example) will produce products for many different markets and segments.

The **marketing mix** consists of the so-called 'Four Ps':

'P':	Product	Price	Promotion	Place
Key elements:	Product mix Product life cycle Product differentiation	Pricing decisions: skimming or penetration pricing	Advertising Sales promotion Personal selling	Channels of distribution

The 'product' consists of both goods and services. Many firms market more than one product. They must consider their **product mix** when planning advertising, pricing and other marketing strategies.

Any product has a limited life. The stages in its **life cycle** are:

● **introduction**: it is introduced on to the market, with low sales but plenty of promotion;

● **growth**: consumer loyalty develops, sales increase and profits start to be made;

● **maturity**: growth slows and the firm uses various techniques to extend the product's life;

● **decline**: total sales and profits fall as the market becomes saturated or new products take over.

Ways of extending product life include the 'new, improved' approach to change its image, introducing new models, and extending the product into other formats (for example, the development of washing powder into a liquid form).

**REVISION
SUMMARY**

Product branding allows product **differentiation** to take place. The brand allows customers to distinguish between near-identical products, encourages them to develop brand loyalty and also makes it possible for the producer to advertise the product.

Organisations must **price** their products. Pricing decisions will be influenced by costs of production (the firm will typically set a price which covers costs and includes a profit element). There are two main **market-led pricing policies**.

● **Skimming**: this is a high-price or 'creaming' strategy, often used when a completely new product is launched. The producer has a temporary monopoly and can, therefore, charge a higher price until competitors start to sell similar products.

● **Penetration**: this strategy involves lower prices and profit margins (for example, to increase market share) and is often used with high-volume and long-life products.

Firms **promote** their products in order to increase sales of existing products, to introduce new products and to compete with other firms. **Advertising** seeks to inform people about – and/or persuade them to buy – the firm's products. **Informative** approaches provide facts and figures about the product. **Persuasive** approaches use tempting images in attempts to convince consumers that they must have the product. Popular media used include commercial TV and radio, and print-based media such as magazines, newspapers and posters. To select a suitable medium the advertiser will balance **cost** and **effectiveness** against **coverage**.

Sales promotion and personal selling – sometimes called 'below-the-line' promotion – are other methods used to push products. **Sales promotion** techniques include free samples, price cutting, competitions and after-sales service. **Personal selling** has an advantage over advertising in that it can target its message at a particular customer: it is not impersonal (but is much more expensive, however).

Marketers must establish how their products and services will reach the marketplace. Decisions involving **place** include having to identify the most appropriate **channel of distribution** for the firm.

If you need to
revise this
subject more
thoroughly,
see the relevant
topics in the
*Letts GCSE
Business
Studies
Study Guide.*

1 One of the 'Four Ps' of the marketing mix is:

  (a) profit   (b) production   (c) personnel   (d) place.

     Answer: ....   (1)

2 Suggest **one** appropriate advertising medium for each of the following:

  (a) A sale of second-hand items, to be held in a village hall.

  ....

  (b) Orange juice, sold in one supermarket chain under its 'own-brand' name.

  ....

  (c) A new GCSE Business Studies textbook.

  ....

  (d) A used car.

  .... (4)

3 *GreenScene* is a firm making 'environmentally friendly' toiletry products. Its owners plan to market a new range of deodorants under the brand name 'Caring Clean'. These deodorants will compete with several other brands already on the market. The owners plan to establish quickly a high market share for the 'Caring Clean' brand.

    The Marketing Manager of *GreenScene* has been asked to suggest whether skimming or penetration pricing should be used for the 'Caring Clean' range. He has also been asked to identify a suitable way to promote this new range.

  (a) Explain why branding is important to *GreenScene*.

  ....

  .... (2)

  (b) Explain the terms:

    (i) *Skimming* ....

    ....

    (ii) *Penetration pricing* ....

    .... (4)

(c) Suggest which of the two approaches should be used in this situation. Give reasons for your answer.

....

....

....

.... (3)

(d) How might the Marketing Manager of *GreenScene* use advertising to market the 'Caring Clean' range? In your answer, explain whether informative and/or persuasive advertising approaches should be used.

....

....

....

....

....

....

....

.... (8)

(e) (i) Identify **two** sales promotion methods that could also be used in marketing the new range.

1. ....

2. .... (2)

(ii) Select **one** of these methods and describe how it could be used to promote the new range.

....

....

....

.... (4)

4 A large firm, which makes gardening equipment, has recently developed a new lawnmower. It was expensive to develop as it is a completely new design.

(a) (i) Suggest **two** pricing policies the firm could use to price its new lawnmower.

1 .... (1)

2 .... (1)

(ii) Select **one** of these pricing policies and explain why you think the firm should use it to price the new lawmnower.

Pricing policy selected: ....

Reason: ....

....

....

.... (2)

The firm wishes to promote its new lawnmower to the public.

(b) (i) State **two** laws which will make the firm careful about what it says about its new lawnmower.

1 .... (1)

2 .... (1)

(ii) Explain **two** methods the firm could use to promote the new lawnmower to the public.

1 ....

.... (2)

2 ....

.... (2)

(c) Describe **one** channel of distribution to the consumer which the firm could use for the lawnmower.

....

....

.... (2)

(d) Explain why the Advertising Standards Authority (ASA) may become interested in the way the firm advertises its new lawnmower.

....

....

.... (2)

The Consumers' Association decides to test the firm's new lawnmower, along with lawnmowers made by the firm's competitors.

(e) (i) Explain **one** reason why the **firm** might be concerned about this test.

....

....

....

.... (2)

(ii) Explain **one** reason why the **consumer** might be pleased about this test.

....

....

....

.... (2)

The firm decides to work out the break-even point for the new lawnmower.

(f) What would this break-even point tell the firm?

....

....

.... (2)

The firm makes some improvements to the new lawnmower.

(g) Give the full name of the department in the firm which would have suggested and tested ideas about these improvements.

.... (1)

These improvements increase the cost of production of the lawnmower but the firm decides not to increase the price of the lawnmower.

(h) (i) Explain the effect this decision would have on the break-even point.

....

.... (2)

(ii) Give **one** reason why the firm may have decided not to increase the price of the lawnmower.

....

.... (2)

NICCEA 1998

5 (a) Elegant Kitchens is a manufacturer of kitchen units. The graph on the next page shows the product life cycle for its 'Farmhouse' range of kitchens. This range has been sold mainly to higher income people.

Product Life Cycle – Farmhouse Kitchen Range

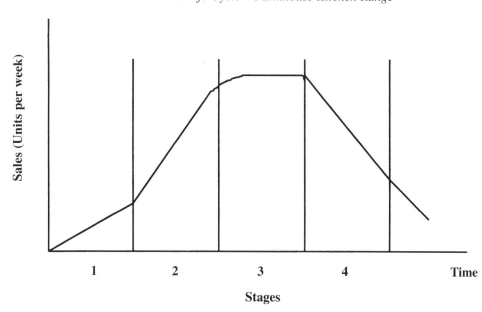

Describe what happens to the sales of the kitchen range during each stage of the product life cycle.

Stage 1 ....

....

Stage 2 ....

....

Stage 3 ....

....

Stage 4 ....

.... (4)

(b) Each of the stages in the product life cycle has a name. Match up the stages with the correct name from this list – decline, maturity, introduction, growth. The last stage has been done for you.

Stage	Name
1	_____
2	_____
3	_____
4	decline	(3)

(c) (i) State and explain **two** methods of market research the firm could use to find out about who might buy the kitchens.

1...

....

2...

.... (4)

(ii) Give **three** questions which could be included in the market research.

1. ....

....

2. ....

....

3. ....

.... (3)

(d) How could Elegant Kitchens increase the sales of its kitchen units?

....

....

....

....

....

....

....

....

....

.... (10)

MEG (specimen)

Many of the GCSE Business Studies questions you have attempted come from case study-type examination papers. In these papers you are typically provided with information about one firm, with the data response type of questions relating to the firm's owners, employees, activities and products. This makes the examination more realistic because the questions are based on a 'real' business situation. This approach also gives examiners the opportunity to set questions drawn from more than one syllabus area.

There are two particularly important points to consider when attempting questions from this style of examination paper, which have already been explained. First, you must remember that, to answer these questions successfully, **any general points made must be related to the particular situation** described in the case study. Second, questions which are made up of parts drawn from different areas of your syllabus mean that you must be able to **integrate your thoughts and ideas.** The logic behind this is that since the different elements of business do not operate in isolation from each other, you should be able to demonstrate that you understand how these business concepts, ideas and functions link together.

*Try to complete the paper in one sitting of **three hours**.*

CASE STUDY: HADLINGTON

The town of Hadlington has grown in recent years. Its population is now 150 000. The local council expects the population to continue increasing, and the age structure of the residents of Hadlington is also expected to change.

Hadlington contains three leisure centres. One of these is operated by Leisuretime plc. The other two are owned and run by the local council. One of the council leisure centres is called the Oakley Leisure Centre. It has a reception desk, a small café area where drinks and snacks are served; a small shop selling swimwear and fitness clothes; a swimming pool; a room containing fitness equipment; a room used for aerobics; and changing rooms.

All local council employees can join the Hadlington 'leisure for pleasure' scheme. This scheme allows these employees to use the leisure facilities at reduced prices in off-peak times. Some local employers, on behalf of their firms, are negotiating with the council to see if this scheme could be extended to their firms' employees.

Oakley Leisure Centre staff have to meet several financial objectives. One of these objectives is to make a 10% return on capital employed.

The staff are also encouraged to hire out the facilities where possible. Therefore, they have started offering 'Friday fun nights', when local teenagers can use the swimming pool and other facilities. Local residents, however, have objected to this development on the grounds of increased noise.

The full-time staff at the leisure centre are themselves concerned about an increasing number of customer complaints. These complaints tend to be about either the clothes sold in the shop area or about the equipment being used in the fitness room.

1 (a) Complete each sentence. Circle the **ONE** word giving the best answer.

(i) The Oakley Leisure Centre is in the .... sector of the economy.

   primary   *secondary*   *tertiary*

(ii) Council employees receive a monthly ....

   debit   *salary*   *profit*

(iii) The full-time employees of Oakley Leisure Centre undergo an annual ....

   mark-up   *appraisal*   *dividend*

(iv) Fitness equipment used at the Oakley Leisure Centre is an example of ....

   debtors   *assets*   *shares*

(v) Oakley Leisure Centre communicates with its customers by ....

   letter   *memorandum*   *e-mail*   (5)

(b) Select the best answer by writing the letter A, B, C or D in the space provided.

(i) The abbreviation 'plc' indicates that Leisuretime plc is a

   A private limited company

   B private limited corporation

   C public limited company

   D public limited corporation   Answer ....

(ii) An example of Leisuretime plc's short-term borrowing is its

   A bank overdraft

   B debentures

   C ordinary shares

   D preference shares   Answer ....

(iii) The directors of Leisuretime plc are appointed by the

   A bank

   B council

   C government

   D shareholders   Answer ....

Letts

Q&A

(iv) The taxation paid by Leisuretime plc on its profits is

A corporation tax

B income tax

C purchase tax

D value added tax   Answer ....

(v) Individuals working for Leisuretime plc have their working terms and conditions stated in the

A articles of association

B contract of employment

C curriculum vitae

D statement of account   Answer ....

(5)

2 (a) Explain how Hadlington Council and local employers may benefit from offering subsidised leisure facilities to their employees.

....

....

....

....

.... (5)

(b) Describe other ways that these employers may improve staff morale without giving a pay increase.

....

....

....

.... (5)

3 (a) Suggest ways in which the local council might promote its 'Friday fun nights'.

....

....

....

....

.... (5)

(b) Explain how the local residents might take appropriate action to influence the Leisure Centre's policies, especially with regard to the 'Friday fun nights'.

....

....

....

....

.... (5)

4 Leisuretime plc owns and operates a large number of leisure centres throughout the UK. Explain how this organisation might benefit from economies of scale.

....

....

....

....

....

....

....

....

.... (10)

5 Mrs Stewart recently bought a sweatshirt from Oakley Leisure Centre. The sweatshirt was sold to her by Kordell, who works part-time at the Centre on Saturdays. After washing the sweatshirt for the first time, Mrs Stewart found that it had shrunk so much that it would no longer fit her. She took it back to Kordell, who did not know what to do in this situation.

(a) (i) Name and describe briefly **one** Act of Parliament which influences the relationship between the Leisure Centre and its customers.

....

....

.... (3)

(ii) Explain whether this Act applies to the situation involving Mrs Stewart.

....

....

.... (3)

(b) Assess the action which the staff at Oakley Leisure Centre might take to reduce the number of customer complaints.

....

....

....

....

....

....

....

....

.... (8)

(c) Suggest ways in which the council and/or the Leisure Centre staff might help part-time staff like Kordell to manage a similar situation in the future.

....

....

....

....

....

....

....

.... (6)

6 The council's accounting staff have calculated the Oakley Leisure Centre's sales this year as follows (last year's figures are shown in brackets).

	Café area	Shop area	Aerobics/ fitness rooms	Swimming pool	Total
Sales (£ 000)	18 (10)	12 (20)	90 (50)	120 (120)	240 (200)

The centre has made a profit of £12 000 this year (the same as last year).
This year's capital employed is £250 000, with current assets of £30 000 and current liabilities of £20 000.

(a) Explain the extent to which the business objectives of Hadlington council may differ from those of Leisuretime plc.

....

....

....

....

....

....

.... (6)

(b) (i) Has the Oakley Centre met its 10% target? Show your workings.

....

....

.... (2)

(ii) Calculate **one** other profitability ratio and **one** liquidity ratio for this Centre.

....

....

....

....

.... (4)

(c) Identify and examine the effect on Oakley Leisure Centre of **one** important trend suggested by the above figures.

....

....

....

....

....

....

....

....

....

....

.... (8)

7

Age	Population, year 2000 (% of total)	Population, year 2010 (% of total)
0–10	9	14
11–20	15	11
21–30	17	12
31–40	15	10
41–50	14	14
51–64	14	18
65 and over	16	21

Planning officials employed by the local council expect the population of Hadlington to increase by a further 8% by the year 2010.

Their calculations suggest that the town's age structure will alter as shown above.

(a) Calculate Hadlington's expected population in the year 2010.

....

.... (2)

(b) (i) Analyse the expected changes in the age structure of Hadlington's population.

....

....

....

....

....

....

.... (6)

(ii) Examine how the Leisure Centre might respond to these expected changes.

....

....

....

....

....

....

....

....

....

....

....

....

....

....

....

....

....

.... (12)

Answers

1 THE BUSINESS ENVIRONMENT

Question	Answer	Mark
1	Advantage: greater efficiency and expertise leads to increased output.	2
	Disadvantage: a need to retrain or even dismiss the employee if the specialised skill becomes out of date.	2

Examiner's tip When answering 'Advantage and Disadvantage' type questions, make sure you check who or what the advantage and disadvantage refers to (in this case it refers to the company, not to the employee).

Question	Answer	Mark
2	**(i)** Holidays taken by French tourists in Wales.	1
	(ii) A South American ship insured with Lloyds of London.	1

Examiner's tip Remember that 'invisibles' refer to services and not goods. When UK citizens take holidays abroad, these are classified as imports and not exports.

Question	Answer	Mark
3	The amount of competition in the area.	1
	Expected number of customers.	1
4 **(a)**	Correct phrases are *public limited company* and *private sector*.	2
(b)	Correct term is *relocation*.	1
5 **(a)**	Cannit Ltd is in the secondary sector; local authorities are in the tertiary sector.	2
(b)	Cannit Ltd is in the private sector; local authorities are in the public sector.	2
(c)	The directors will consider the **nature of the new site**.	1
	Is the rent higher or lower than at present? Will any modifications be required to the buildings? Will expansion be possible?	2
	Second, the directors will consider the **views of their existing employees**.	1

Question	Answer	Mark
	For example, they will wish to discover how many of the present workforce will be prepared to relocate. This enables them to identify if workers with key skills will be lost to the company. The costs associated with moving employees will need to be calculated.	2
	Third, the directors will study the transport networks at the new site.	1
	Will they be better or worse than those at the existing site? Are other transport methods available for the new site? The directors will therefore assess whether transport costs will rise or fall, and whether transport efficiency will improve overall.	2
	A fourth area for the directors to consider is associated with **the need to employ new staff** at the new site.	1
	Will new employees be available with suitable skills and experience? If so, what pay levels will they be expecting from the company, and will the company be prepared to meet them? If any training is required, will the company be able to provide it or are there locally based training schemes that can be used?	2
(d)	The directors might face the problem of losing existing staff who are suitably skilled and experienced. They face the problem of a **lack of geographical mobility** of labour: not all staff – possibly very few – will be prepared to move to another part of the country because of family and other ties. The result is that the company's efficiency and competitiveness will be reduced until new employees become as efficient as existing ones.	2
	A second problem the directors face is **financing the relocation**. The costs of the move will have to be met, and the directors may have to borrow (and therefore pay interest on the amount borrowed) to meet these costs.	2
	A third problem for the directors is **to inform existing customers and suppliers** about the move. Steps need to be taken to let relevant people and organisations know that the company is moving. They may even find that some customers will be less willing to trade with them if the move is likely to lead to longer delivery journeys, and that suppliers add increased transport costs to the cost of the items being supplied.	2

Examiner's tip Remember that if a question asks you to explain something, you must expand the points you make; don't simply list them.

Question	Answer	Mark
(e)	Telford: there are lower costs (evidence of rent, and a lower wage area) and a larger workforce (higher population) which is more likely to possess relevant skills (experienced in manufacturing industry).	2
	Dover: it is better placed for Europe and exporting generally (on coast, close to Channel Tunnel), and is closer to suppliers.	2

2 ORGANISATION OF BUSINESS

Question	Answer	Mark
1	The name of the company is followed by the letters 'plc'.	1
	Shares are sold on the Stock Exchange.	1
	They have limited liability.	1
2	Sole trader: (a) and (d).	2
	Partnership: (c) and (g).	2
	Private limited company: (e) and (f).	2
	PLC: (b) and (h).	2

3 (a) One reason the owners should operate as a limited company is that they receive the benefit of **limited liability**. The owners will invest capital in the company: the idea of limited liability is that they are only responsible for meeting business debts from this business investment. In other words, the owners only risk losing the amount of capital they have agreed to invest in the company, and they cannot be forced to use personal savings to meet any business debts. Most partners have unlimited liability, and are therefore not protected in the same way. **2**

A second reason is that a limited company is a **separate legal entity** or 'person'. The law regards a company as being separate from its owners, which is not the case with a partnership. This brings the advantage that – if one of the owners dies, retires or leaves – the company can still continue (unlike a partnership, which must be dissolved and reformed if a partner leaves). Because it is a separate 'person', the company can enter contracts and take legal action in its own name, unlike a partnership. **2**

> **Examiner's tip** Oakwell is a *private* limited company, so be careful not to include advantages more clearly associated with a PLC, such as economies of scale or being able to sell shares to the public at large.

(b) The term 'limited' warns traders with Oakwell that, if the company fails and as a result owes them money, **they may not have their debts paid**. This is because the owners have limited liability, and traders cannot make them use personal assets (such as savings) to meet the company's business debts. In practice, therefore, traders check a company's financial position before letting it build up large debts through buying from them on credit. **2**

(c) The term 'PLC' stands for **public limited company**. It is one of two forms of limited company, the word 'public' referring to the fact that – unlike a private company – a PLC can approach the general public to become shareholders by buying shares in it. **2**

Answers to Unit 2

Question	Answer	Mark

Examiner's tip The question expects you to explain briefly the meaning of the term PLC, and not simply to state what the initials stand for.

(d) The advantage of remaining a private company is that the company's financial affairs can be **kept more private**: PLCs have to disclose far more information through publishing their accounts. The other owner also realises that it is **extremely costly** to become a PLC, and that they **risk losing control** through a takeover bid launched by another company.

2

Examiner's tip You must remember that the advantages of remaining private outweigh those of 'going public'. Most companies remain private.

(e) Memorandum: this explains how the company relates to the **outside world.**

1

Its main items include a Name clause and an Objects clause (explaining for what purpose the company was created).

1

Articles: this explains how the company operates **internally.**

1

For example, the Articles contain details about directors and meetings.

1

(f) One difference is that a PLC is owned by **shareholders** which are other companies and/or members of the general public who have chosen to invest in the PLC. A public corporation is owned by **people at large** since it is a state organisation.

2

A second difference is that a PLC is controlled by its **Board of Directors**. Public corporations are controlled through an appointed Board, but also through **Parliament** (the Cabinet, various Ministers, and MPs' questions) and **consultative committees.**

2

Examiner's tip Be careful with the terms 'public' and 'private'. Public companies are in the private sector, not the public sector.

4 (a) A monopoly is a **single supplier** of a product or service. It tends, therefore, to have complete control of its pricing and other marketing policies. Firms in more competitive markets are normally not price setters, but price takers: less efficient firms will be forced out of business.

2

Examiner's tip The question refers to privatised monopolies, but you can recall and use points relating to state-owned monopolies in your answer.

(b) The government seeks to control monopolies so that the buyers of the monopoly's goods or services are **not unfairly exploited**. This situation could occur if the monopoly took advantage of its position as the only supplier by, for example, setting very high prices.

2

Letts
Q&A

Question	Answer	Mark
(c)	Where the monopolist is a 'natural' monopoly – such as water or power – a single controller can **organise the supply of this item for the benefit of the consumer**. If the item was supplied by many different firms, there may be over-supply in some (profitable) areas and under supply in other (non-profitable) ones.	2
(d)	'Privatisation' refers to selling public sector assets to the private sector. This takes place by converting public corporations to PLC status (for example British Gas plc), or by the government selling off its shares in public corporations (such as BT plc).	2

Examiner's tip It is often useful to include a brief real-life example in your answer.

Question	Answer	Mark
(e)	For: Privatisation can **increase competition** by breaking up a monopoly. Greater competition should lead to greater efficiency and lower prices.	2
	Against: **Private monopolies often result** from privatisation. It is less easy to control and regulate a private monopoly than one in the public sector.	2

Examiner's tip To ensure you get both marks for each part of the question, make a basic statement and then expand it, explaining its relevance.

Question		Answer	Mark
(f)	**(i)**	Privatisation **raises revenue** for the government through the sale of public sector assets. The government can then use this extra revenue for investment or other long-term purposes.	1
	(ii)	The firms can become more efficient through streamlining and being in a **more competitive market**.	1
	(iii)	Consumers benefit from the **greater efficiency and lower prices** that should result from the privatisation: there should be a greater choice of products and services.	1

Question		Answer	Mark
5 (a)		Hash is likely to have been motivated by the **desire to be his own boss**. As a sole trader, he will both own and control the business, receiving all the profits himself.	2
(b)	**(i)**	Hash is called a **franchisee**.	1
	(ii)	The company is known as the **franchisor**.	1
(c)		One advantage to Hash of taking out a franchise is that **he receives the support of the franchisor**: this can include national advertising, individual training and consultancy services, as well as equipment.	1
		A second advantage is that Hash will be selling a **recognised product** which will have a good reputation nationally.	1
		One disadvantage is that Hash **loses control** over what he can sell and often how he can sell it: he is no longer his own boss.	1
		A second disadvantage is **that he must pay a certain percentage** of his income to the franchisor. He will still probably be working long hours, but will no longer be able to keep all the profits for himself.	1

Question	Answer	Mark

Because a franchisee and a traditional sole trader are quite similar in operation, you need to identify key differences, such as what each sells and how each is supported.

(d) **(i)** Hash will want to **survive** in business, and **compete successfully with local competitors** in order to establish an acceptable level of turnover. **2**

(ii) The franchisor will also see **survival** as an important business objective: it may seek to achieve this objective in a similar way to Hash by, for example, providing a competitive product (on a national basis, compared with the local scale of Hash). **2**

Second, the franchisor may wish to **expand** through increasing its market share (again on a national, rather than a local, basis). **2**

It is quite acceptable to use the same objectives for both parts. If you do so, remember to explain the different ways that a franchisor and franchisee achieve each objective.

3 BUSINESS FINANCE AND GROWTH

Question	Answer	Mark

1 The first factor could be the **cost** of the loan: what rate of interest is to be charged? Owners will need this information in order to budget for the cost of the finance. **2**

The second factor could be the **repayment** period involved: is short-term or long-term finance involved, and is there an agreed repayment date or is it open-ended? Owners require this information to assess whether the source is appropriate. **2**

The final factor could be the **availability** of the finance: is an internal source available, or must it be external finance? Owners need information about all relevant sources and their availability in order to make the most informed decision. **2**

Relate your answers to why owners need this information: decision-making will be involved in each case.

2 The answer is (c): they are in the same area of work and at the same stage of production. **1**

3 The rate of interest represents the **cost of borrowing**. The higher the rate of interest, the more expensive the finance and, therefore, the lower the firm's profits. **2**

Question	Answer	Mark
4 (a)	Overdraft: The partners do not know exactly how much will be needed, and an overdraft is **flexible**: interest is payable on the actual amount of the overdraft, so the partners will not have to pay interest on an amount they do not need.	2
	Loan: the loan will be for a **fixed sum**, at a fixed rate of interest and for a fixed period: this is appropriate where the partners know the amount they need, and will allow them to calculate accurately whether they can afford the loan.	2

Examiner's tip You must relate the characteristics of overdrafts and loans to this particular situation. One item (materials) involves a varying cost, whereas the cost of the machine is known with greater certainty.

Question	Answer	Mark
(b)	Materials could be bought on **trade credit**.	1
	This source is closely associated with buying materials, and may even enable the partners to manufacture and sell the products before having to pay for the materials (which would therefore be paid from sale proceeds). The disadvantage is that it is not easy to obtain trade credit as a new firm, and even if it is obtained the partners would have to lose the chance of receiving discounts from suppliers for prompt payments.	2
	Leasing arrangements could be made for the machine.	1
	It may be possible to lease it and avoid a large financial outlay. One disadvantage is that leasing can mean the partners face a continuing regular cost for a machine they do not own. Credit sale or hire purchase are possible variations here.	2

Examiner's tip Examining the difference between the nature of payments for the materials – varying amounts which must be paid for almost daily – and the machine (a possible 'one-off' cost) helps you choose appropriate sources.

Question	Answer	Mark
5 (a) (i)	Multinational: an organisation which **produces in more than one country**.	1
	Conglomerate: an organisation which is **involved in more than one industry**.	1
	Diversify: to move into **other areas of work** and business activity.	1
(ii)	1. Horizontal: '...took over another oil refining company...'	1
	2. Vertical: '...now owns several petrol station chains...'	1
	3. Lateral: '...as well as hotels and entertainment complexes...'	1
(b)	Multinational corporations are **PLCs**.	1
(c)	A company now has **greater control over its prices**: by integrating with suppliers and/or outlets, the profits of the previous suppliers/outlets now belong to the firm. It can absorb them to give greater flexibility over its price policy.	2

Answers to Unit 3

Question	Answer	Mark

Examiner's tip Consider how a company's position improves compared with its competitors, when vertical integration takes place. You need to explain that it can benefit financially by taking over some of the production stages.

(d) £8000: A **mortgage loan** would be appropriate because it is long term, associated with property, and payments can be budgeted for. — 2

£1500: A **bank loan** is suitable, since Joan can negotiate not only the amount borrowed, but also the payment level and the length of the loan. — 2

£500: An **overdraft** would be appropriate because variable amounts will be needed (stock levels will be influenced by seasonal factors) and this is a flexible method of borrowing. — 2

Examiner's tip There isn't only one right answer here: a number of appropriate sources exist, and you will receive full marks so long as you relate the source to the amount and the situation.

6 (a) Ian might have wanted to become his own boss. He does not have to share his profits with others and might enjoy the independence of working for himself. Working for oneself can be highly motivating and rewarding. — 5

(b) (i) Ian's major business objective in the early years would probably have been survival. He would be particularly interested in it meeting set liquidity targets. Ian would be more concerned about establishing a niche market for himself on which he could build, rather than seeking to maximise profits. He would also have wanted to gradually increase his market share. — 6

(ii) As Ian's business became more established, he would become more interested in its profitability. Although still concerned about liquidity, a higher return on capital employed would become more important. With an established business, Ian may also wish to become more aggressive in marketing and, therefore, expand his business's market share (he is concentrating on turnover). By widening his product range, Ian is making his business safer through this greater diversification. — 8

Examiner's tip You need to recognise the business objective of survival is of more concern to an entrepreneur at the start. When the business is established, he or she can afford to be more concerned about profitability and market share.

(c) The major risk Ian faces in running his own business is that of limited liability. if his business fails, he becomes liable to meet all the risk for all business debts from his personal wealth. Ian also faces the risk for all businesses, i.e. that of uncertainty. He is unsure of the level of demand for his products. Other common business risks, such as fire damage and theft, are insurable. — 6

Question	Answer	Mark
(d)	Ian would have wanted to obtain long-term finance. Share issues to the public are not an option for a sole trader, so he might have sought a long-term loan/mortgage from a lender, such as a commercial bank. This has the advantage of relative certainty (the length of the loan is agreed and the interest payments are known, subject to any change in rates). Shorter-term finance could have been obtained through agreeing an overdraft facility with his bank, obtaining necessary equipment through leasing or credit sale agreements, and through Ian using 'trade credit' (e.g. taking advantage of the credit terms offered by his suppliers). Given his need for long-term financial investment, I would probably recommend that Ian take out a long-term loan from a reputable financial institution, such as a high street bank.	**12**

Examiner's tip | Be careful to distinguish between long-term and short-term finance.

4 PRODUCTION

Question	Answer	Mark
1	The answer is (b) ships: the other three are more closely associated with batch or mass forms.	**1**
2	Payment for machinery.	**1**
	The cost of buying vans.	**1**
	Rates.	**1**

Examiner's tip | The key question is: which costs don't change as output changes? These are the fixed costs, which we then select as the answers.

3 (a)	The variable cost of 10 units = £3550 − £3400 = £150: the variable cost of each unit is, therefore, £15.	**2**

Examiner's tip | You must remember that the extra cost of producing more units will be a variable cost, because fixed costs don't change as output increases.

(b)	Average cost $= \dfrac{£3400}{500}$	**1**
	$= £6.80$ per unit.	**1**

4 (a)	The batch method of production involves the company in **making a quantity** of 'Sucker' cleaners **without using a continuous production process**. After one batch has been made, production switches to another product. The factory production area is often organised by grouping similar machines, equipment and processes together.	**2**

Question	Answer	Mark

(b) The directors may not use mass production methods because the **demand** for this vacuum cleaner may be too low to let them make it on a continuous basis. Mass production is found where the product has a very high and a long-term level of demand.   2

(c) The table suggests that, as production increases from 10 000 to 20 000, costs per cleaner fall from £65 to £55.   2

This trend continues: if 30 000 are made and sold, costs per cleaner fall to £50.   2

(d) **(i)** **Purchasing** economies can occur when a firm increases its output. The directors will find they receive better bulk-buying discounts and more favourable credit terms from their suppliers as they buy more components and raw materials for their cleaners.   2

(ii) **Marketing** economies: the directors need to advertise and promote their cleaners. If they spread these marketing costs across a greater number of machines, they will reduce the unit cost of marketing.   2

(e) The lowest unit costs exist at an output of 30 000 units (£50). Above this level of output the company seems to be experiencing **diseconomies of scale**: unit costs rise to £55.   1

If we calculate the profit at these output levels, we have:

$30\ 000 \times £15\ (65 - 50) = £450\ 000$ 1

$40\ 000 \times £10\ (65 - 55) = £400\ 000$ 1

The company makes a higher profit at an output of 30 000.   1

5 (a) **(i)** Calculate by multiplying the number of dresses by £700.

Dresses	Revenue (£)
0	0
50	35 000
100	70 000
150	105 000
200	140 000
250	175 000

1

Question	Answer	Mark
	(ii) See the following graph.	**3**

Examiner's tip The Total Costs line is sometimes labelled Variable Costs when displayed like this.

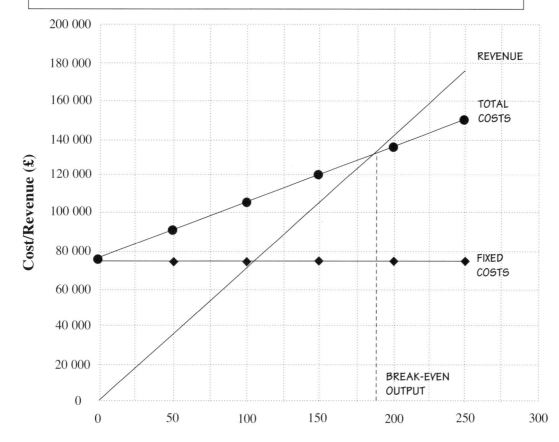

	(iii) See the graph above.	**1**
	(iv) 187 or 188 dresses.	**1**

Examiner's tip The answer can be checked by calculation. Contribution is £700 (sales price) less £300 variable costs (£15 000/50) = £400. Divided into £75 000 Fixed Costs gives a break-even point of 187.5 dresses.

(b)	**(i)**	Fixed costs **stay the same as output changes.**	**1**
		An example is **rent** of premises.	**1**
	(ii)	Variable costs **change in proportion to changes in output.**	**1**
		An example is the cost of **raw materials.**	**1**
(c)	**(i)**	Job production involves making a product (a dress in this case) as a 'one-off' item to **customer specifications.**	**2**
	(ii)	Batch production involves making a **certain number** (a 'batch') of the **same item** on a production line, then switching the line to manufacture a batch of a different product.	**2**
		Flow or 'mass' production is where a production line is devoted exclusively to one particular process or product; it is made **continuously.**	**2**

Answers to Unit 4

Question	Answer	Mark

Examiner's tip Make sure that your answer explains the difference in the number made and points out that flow production is continuous in nature.

(iii) The employees may be **demotivated** as a result of the change; they may face **de-skilling**, where individual skills are lost because they are no longer used. The employees may also face **redundancy**: batch and flow production is less labour intensive than job production, relying more on the use of machinery. If not made redundant, they will probably face **re-training**, to become used to new machines. **4**

---

6 (a)
$$\text{Break-even point} = \frac{£3600}{£5}$$ **1**

= 720 photographs. **1**

Workings: total yearly fixed costs = (£100 rent + £200 wages) x 12 = £3600.

unit contribution = sales price less variable cost = £6 – (20p + 30p + 50p) = £5.

Examiner's tip A question may give you monthly and annual information. In this case, you must convert the monthly figures to yearly ones.

(b)

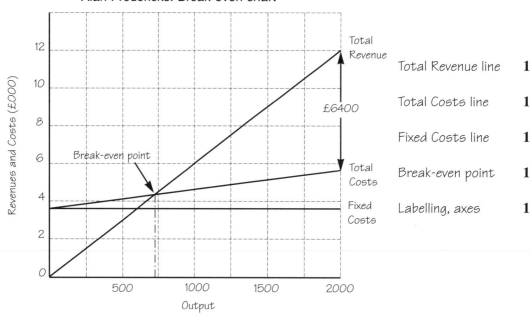

Alan Fredericks: Break-even chart

Total Revenue line	1
Total Costs line	1
Fixed Costs line	1
Break-even point	1
Labelling, axes	1

(c)
- **(i)** 720 — 1
- **(ii)** £4320 — 1
- **(iii)** £6400 — 1
- **(iv)** Profit of £1400 — 1
- **(v)** 1280 — 1

Question	Answer	Mark

(d)	If Alan drops the price to £5, this will change his profit, break-even point and margin of safety.	1
	His new contribution is now only £4 (£5 – £1), which gives a break-even point of 900 photos (£3600 divided by £4). Alan will have a better margin of safety, of 1600 photographs (2500 – 900).	3
	At sales of 2500, Alan's total income will be £12 500 but his total costs are now £6100– made up of £3600 fixed (these do not change as he alters his selling price) and £2500 variable (£1 x 2500 units: the unit variable cost also doesn't change). This gives him an expected profit of £6400, the same figure when his selling price was £6.	3
	On this evidence I would not recommend Alan to drop his price to £5. Although his profit should remain the same and he has a greater margin of safety (1600 and not 1280) before he ceases to make a profit, he now has to sell more photographs (900 and not 720) before he breaks even.	3

5 ACCOUNTING

Question	Answer	Mark
1	Gross Profit $\dfrac{75\,000 \times 100}{300\,000}$ Sales	1
	Gross Profit Margin is 25%.	1
	Net Profit $\dfrac{30\,000 \times 100}{300\,000}$ Sales	1
	Net Profit Margin is 10%.	1

2		Revenue	Capital	
	Purchase of new computer system.		✔	1
	Rental fee paid for new photocopier.	✔		1
	Sales office staff salaries.	✔		1
	Cost of new factory extension.		✔	1
	Purchase of new delivery vehicle.		✔	1
	Petrol costs for the delivery vehicle.	✔		1

Question	Answer	Mark

3 (a) 1. Gross Profit is the difference between the company's **sales** and its **cost of sales**. It shows how much profit Bubbles (UK) Ltd has made by taking the cost of making its leisure wear from the sales value of these products. **2**

2. Net Profit is the difference between **all revenues** and **all expenses**; it is the Gross Profit less other office and selling costs, such as advertising, office salaries and distribution expenses. **2**

(b) 1993: Sales £200 000 – Cost of Sales £120 000 **1**

= Gross Profit £80 000. **1**

1994: Sales £250 000 – Gross Profit £100 000 **1**

= Cost of Sales £150 000. **1**

(c) Net Profit = Gross Profit – Expenses

= £80 000 – £50 000 **1**

= £30 000. **1**

(d) (i) A firm's rate of turnover refers to the **speed at which it sells its stock**. We calculate the number of times average stock is sold in a trading period and express this as the 'rate of turnover'. **2**

(ii) Opening stock £25 000: closing stock £15 000

$$\text{Average stock} = \frac{£25\ 000 + £15\ 000}{2} = £20\ 000$$ **1**

$$\text{Rate of turnover} = \frac{\text{Cost of Sales}}{\text{Average Stock}} = \frac{£120\ 000}{£20\ 000} = 6 \text{ times}$$ **2**

The rate of turnover is therefore 6 times in 1993. Bubbles (UK) Ltd turns its stock over once every two months. **2**

Question	Answer	Mark

It is risky not to show your workings: one simple arithmetical error and you lose all 5 marks. If you do show workings, you may still receive most of the marks for correct method, even if your calculation is wrong.

(iii) 1. Bubbles (UK) Ltd may have spent more money on **advertising**, thereby boosting the sales of its products. **1**

2. It may have faced **reduced competition**, e.g. through a competitor closing down. **1**

3. Bubbles (UK) Ltd may have entered a **new market** (or may have started selling a successful new product in one of its existing markets). **1**

(e) **(i)** 1. Ordinary shares receive a **variable dividend**, payable after all the company's other lenders and shareholders have received their interest and dividend payments. **1**

2. Ordinary shares normally grant the owners a **vote** which can be exercised at the Annual General Meeting of Bubbles (UK) Ltd. **1**

(ii) The Fixed Assets figure increased by £50 000 during 1994. The company therefore invested in additional fixed assets. **3**

(iii) 1993: Current Assets less Current Liabilities = nil.

1994: Current Assets less Current Liabilities = £10 000.

The company's Net Current Assets have increased by £10 000, through a £5000 increase in Current Assets and a £5000 fall in Current Liabilities. **3**

The term 'net' in accounting refers to the difference between two totals (as shown here: another illustration is net profit, the difference between gross profit and other expenses). Net Current Assets is another name for Working Capital.

(iv) 1. Additional **Ordinary Shares** could be issued. **1**

2. The company could use some of its **Reserves**. **1**

3. Bubbles (UK) Ltd could take out a **long-term loan** such as a mortgage. **1**

(f) **(i)** 'Capital employed' is a term used to describe the long-term capital (share capital, reserves and long-term loans) used by a company to **resource its activities**. **2**

(ii) 1994 capital employed = Ordinary Share Capital + Reserves = £210 000 **1**

Return on capital employed $= \dfrac{£40\ 000 \times 100}{£210\ 000}$ **1**

$= 19\%$. **1**

(iii) To the shareholder, the return on capital employed indicates the **profitability** of investing in the company. **1**

Question	Answer	Mark
	A high return on capital employed (such as 19% for Bubbles (UK) Ltd) suggests that the company is a potentially **good investment**.	1
	A company making such a return is likely to be in a position to propose and pay a **high dividend** to its shareholders.	1
	Investors in companies with high returns on capital employed may find that their **shares increase in value**.	1

> **Examiner's tip** You can relate the general points about return on capital to your calculations in (ii).

6 HUMAN RELATIONS AND WORK

Question	Answer	Mark
1	(b)	1

2	**Interviewing** job applicants.	1
	Looking after **staff welfare**.	1
	Training staff.	1

3	(a)	(i)	One advantage is that **new ideas** will be brought into the company. Second, a particular **specialist** can be employed which avoids the time and cost of training an existing member of staff.	2

> **Examiner's tip** State the advantages from the company's viewpoint.

		(ii)	The company could use a specialist recruitment agency, or a Job Centre.	2
	(b)	(i)	1. A **tour** of the company's premises.	1
			2. A **talk** on the company's history.	1
			3. **Meetings** with staff from the new employee's department.	1
		(ii)	Osborne Ltd: the new employee starts to make a **contribution** to the company's work as quickly as possible.	1
			Employee: feels wanted (is **motivated**) from the start of being employed by Osborne Ltd.	1
	(c)	(i)	On-the-job training is **internal**, with employees being trained as they work: the instructor is often the post-holder, with training concentrating on specific skills required for the job. Off-the-job training is **external** and is more associated with attending local colleges or specialist training firms.	2

Question	Answer	Mark
(ii)	One reason is that the employee normally gets some form of external certification, e.g. a particular **qualification**. Second, the employee usually gains **wider knowledge and skills** from specialist trainers.	2

> **Examiner's tip** Here you must frame your answer from the point of view of the employee and not of the employer. Put yourself in the employee's 'shoes' to help identify reasons: why might you prefer off-the-job training?

Question	Answer	Mark
4	Sex Discrimination Act; Race Relations Act.	2
5 (a)	1. work location; 2. products/service being sold; 3. hours.	3
(b)	Loss of orders and loss of goodwill, because sales staff act as representatives of the firm	2
(c)	1. lack of information regarding pay; 2. shop window is an unsuitable location for the advert; 3. no indication of the type of experience required; 4. no contact name to accompany the telephone number.	4
(d)	Motivates the new employees from the start; provides them with key skills and information needed; helps them to make an effective contribution from the start of their employment.	4
(e)	The amount received depends on sales made, which therefore does not guarantee a regular income; amount sold may, to a certain extent, be out of the control of the sales team.	2
(f)	Training – to update them with new skills; offer financial and/or non-financial incentives, e.g. company cars, healthcare schemes, subsidised meals.	4
(g)	Workers may be more concerned with other objectives which may partly clash with profit-maximisation objectives (e.g. greater emphasis on service/quality which might affect profit levels).	2
(h)	If Sellit's wages are below the minimum rate, it would lead to pay levels being increased to meet the minimum wage. This in turn could lead to job losses and lower profit margins. Alternatively, it may lead to better trained and more highly motivated staff, improved quality of output and higher customer satisfaction.	4

> **Examiner's tip** We do not know the firm's wage levels, so your answer should relate to both positive and negative aspects of the minimum wage.

Question	Answer	Mark
6 (a)	Many workers are only available for part-time work (e.g. for **domestic** reasons).	2
	It is **less expensive** to recruit and employ part-timers (fewer benefits).	2
	Part-time workers give Rightway Stores more **flexibility** (hours of work).	2

Question	Answer	Mark
(b)	A high turnover of staff means that a lot of Rightway's employees are leaving the company. This leads to **increased costs** of recruitment and selection (e.g. more advertising, time spent interviewing). Also, the new staff will need **training** and induction, and there may also be a **lack of knowledge** about the company's products, store layout and store policy. This may lead to **low morale** amongst the remaining staff.	**8**

> **Examiner's tip** With such questions, it can be a useful tactic to (briefly) define the key term; in this case, staff turnover.

(c)	**(i)** Rightway will need to consider the **cost** of advertising as well as its **coverage**. For example, TV adverts will be inappropriate because of the high cost and wide coverage. **Local radio** is more appropriate: it has local coverage and is not too expensive. The store will consider **Job Centre** advertising which is very inexpensive and is focused in the local area. In addition, **local newspapers** are popular media for advertising local part-time jobs because of their typically high circulation in the region and relatively low cost.	**8**

> **Examiner's tip** Your answer must reflect the fact that the store is looking for part-time workers, so will wish to advertise locally and inexpensively.

	(ii) Suitable methods include face-to-face **interviews**, aptitude **tests** and taking up **references**. The store management will wish to find out a little about the applicants' backgrounds and support (thus the references) and personal skills (e.g. at interview). Because the staff may also deal with money and calculations as well as with people, they may be tested on these skills.	**8**
(d)	I would expect the company to concentrate on a number of areas and issues. The following should motivate new employees.	
	Firstly, they need to be familiar with **store layout** and **key personnel**. They should also meet with their immediate supervisor and perhaps also with other (e.g. full-time) colleagues.	**4**
	The second area in training is **information** on the history and current policies of Rightway Stores. The new employees may, for example, be shown a video on the company and be given a talk by a manager concerning its mission statement and current market position.	**3**
	The final area is **individual training**. I would expect employees to spend time using any machines or equipment they will have to use in their job. They will need to be made aware of Health and Safety and other rules and procedures which affect their work. This training should allow them to work efficiently when they start work in the store itself.	**3**

7 MARKETING

Question	Answer	Mark
1	(d)	1
2 (a)	A series of small **posters** put up in the village.	1
(b)	The supermarket could advertise on regional or national **television**.	1
(c)	**Leaflets** sent by the publisher to schools and teachers.	1
(d)	An advertisement in a **local newspaper**.	1

> **Examiner's tip** Make sure you have chosen a medium that is realistic for the given situation: for example, (a) would not be advertised on television, but (b) could well be.

3 (a)	Branding allows *GreenScene* to **advertise** the new deodorant products by name. It also means that consumers who enjoy the products will buy them again, through their **brand loyalty** to the product.	2
(b) (i)	The term 'skimming' refers to a market-based pricing policy of setting **high prices**: an alternative name for this is 'creaming'.	2
(ii)	'Penetration pricing' refers to another market-based pricing policy, where a firm sets **low prices** in order to establish a strong market position.	2
(c)	I would select **penetration pricing** as the more appropriate policy in this situation.	1
	The evidence suggests that *GreenScene*'s new products are not the first on the market. It is, therefore, not in a position to exploit any market advantage of being the first supplier. Furthermore, the owners want 'a high market share', and the low-price approach of penetration pricing should encourage many people to try the new products.	2
(d)	The Marketing Manager must answer a number of key questions. First, what is **the range of media** available to the firm? The Manager needs to identify the particular market segments in which to advertise, and which media are most suitable for the segments. The medium's cost, its effectiveness and its ability to reach the targeted audience will need consideration. For example, TV reaches a mass audience and is effective (sound, movement and colour), but it may be too expensive for *GreenScene*.	2
	The second question to answer concerns the **style of advertising**. To what extent will it be informative and to what extent will it try to persuade the consumer to buy the products? The 'green' aspects of the range need explaining (informative), but *GreenScene* is competing with established products and will need to convince competitors' customers that they should try these new products (persuasive).	2

Question	Answer	Mark
	A third question is how the **advertising strategy** will be developed. For example, can GreenScene employ a specialist advertising agency to design and launch the advertisements?	2
	A fourth question is how the advertising will link with the other elements in the **marketing mix**: for example, GreenScene's existing sales promotion, channels of distribution and penetration pricing policy.	2

Examiner's tip We can use what we know about the firm and the product in our answer: important points are its likely 'green' selling point, and that it will probably be sold nationally.

Question	Answer	Mark
(e) **(i)**	1. Free samples.	1
	2. Premium offers.	1
(ii)	I would use a **premium offer**. This could involve giving a free gift if the customer collects and keeps (say) labels off the deodorants.	1
	GreenScene might offer to send one free 'Caring Clean' deodorant to a customer who sends in three labels from previous purchases from this range. A different item in the range could be given as the gift. This has the advantage that **repeat purchases are encouraged**, which helps establish brand loyalty. It would also introduce a customer who has bought one product from the range to a different one in this range.	3
4 (a) **(i)**	Skimming (or creaming) and Penetration.	2
(ii)	Skimming (if selected): the firm will have a temporary monopoly before its competitors follow the new design. OR Penetration (if selected): the firm will achieve high sales and discourage competitors from adopting the new design.	2
(b) **(i)**	Sale and Supply of Goods Act.	1
	Consumer Protection Act.	1
(ii)	Advertising campaign: e.g. by TV, mass coverage, pictures showing unique design.	2
	Sales promotion: e.g. price discount coupons in newspapers or linked with firm's other gardening equipment.	2
(c)	Firm to large retailer (to public): traditional wholesalers not appropriate since most lawnmowers are sold in large 'D-I-Y', catalogue and similar stores.	2
(d)	All adverts must be legal, decent, honest and truthful, so the ASA will ensure the firm's adverts meet this standard.	2
(e) **(i)**	Results are published in 'Which?' magazine, and may show the new mower is less efficient than competitors' models.	2
(ii)	Tests are independent of manufacturers and give unbiased information to the consumer on the different models tested.	2

Question	Answer	Mark

(f) The break-even point tells the firm the number of mowers it needs to sell before starting to make a profit. — 2

(g) Research and Development. — 1

(h) **(i)** The break-even point rises because the contribution (selling price less variable costs) per mower falls. — 2

(ii) Increased price means a less competitive position in the market, leading to fewer sales being made. — 2

---

5 (a) Stage 1 During this stage, the range is introduced on to the market, and sales gradually take place. — 1

Stage 2 During this stage, sales of the range take off as it becomes better known. — 1

Stage 3 During this stage, sales reach their maximum level. — 1

Stage 4 During this stage, sales gradually decline as the range reaches the end of its life. — 1

(b) 1. introduction — 1

2. growth — 1

3. maturity — 1

(c) **(i)** 1. **Field research** via questionnaires, either posted to people living in the more expensive housing areas in the locality or completed by doorstep questioning. — 1

The purpose of the questionnaire is to collect information from and about possible customers. — 1

2. **Desk research**. — 1

The purpose here is to study existing information (e.g. from government or trade association publications) about prospective customers. — 1

Question	Answer	Mark
(ii)	1. How long have you lived in your present house? Less than 1 year; between 1 and 3 years; over 3 years.	**1**
	2. Have you had a fitted kitchen installed in this house? Yes/No	**1**
	3. If the answer to the question above is 'Yes', how long ago was this? Within the last year; between 1 and 3 years ago; over 3 years.	**1**
(d)	The owners of Elegant Kitchens will consider the company's **promotion policy** and media: for example, they may decide to advertise using media new to it such as on the local commercial radio station.	**3**
	They can also consider whether this **product range** can be extended (e.g. by using less expensive materials), so that other lower income groups might become interested in buying these units.	**3**
	The owners could decide to cut the **price** of the existing range: although this reduces the profit margin, greater sales may compensate for this.	**2**
	The owners could also review the **places** where the range is presently sold, to see whether there are other suitable outlets for selling the units.	**2**

Examiner's tip   Use your knowledge of the marketing mix to identify possible strategies. Refer to the product, its price, how it is promoted and where it is sold (place).

8 Mock examination paper

Question	Answer	Mark
1 (a) (i)	tertiary	1
(ii)	salary	1
(iii)	appraisal	1
(iv)	assets	1
(v)	letter	1
(b) (i)	C	1
(ii)	A	1
(iii)	D	1
(iv)	A	1
(v)	B	1
2 (a)	Increased motivation: shows employees that they are being thought about.	2
	This leads to better morale and greater efficiency.	1
	Employees may be fitter/less stressed, this also increases efficiency and ouput.	2
(b)	Financial incentives or non-financial incentives can be offered.	2
	Examples include company cars, private healthcare schemes and subsidised travel.	3
3 (a)	The promotion needs to focus on a specific age group (i.e. teenagers).	1
	The promotion must have a local, rather than a regional/national focus.	1
	Examples include local paper advert, leaflet through doors and a poster in the Centre.	3
(b)	Residents should form a pressure group, which is an organised group of people with similar interests who try to influence others.	2
	The pressure group could: meet with the Centre management; contact their local councillors; write to the appropriate council committee/department.	3
4	Economies of scale arise when a firm lowers its average unit costs. Lesiuretime plc may benefit from:	2
	managerial economies (e.g. employing specialist/experienced leisure centre managers);	2
	financial economies (e.g. centralised borrowing agreements);	2
	purchasing economies (e.g. bulk buying of fitness equipment);	2
	marketing economies (e.g. paying lower advertising rates).	2

Answers to mock examination paper

Question	Answer	Mark

> **Examiner's tip** Because this question makes you apply your knowledge, choose those economies of scale which you can relate most easily to a leisure centre.

5 (a) (i) Sale and Supply of Goods Act 1994. **1**

Under this Act, goods must be of satisfactory quality (fit to be sold), fit for their intended purpose, and (if sold by description) matching the description given. **2**

(ii) Yes. **1**

She has bought goods (not received a service) which should, therefore, be of satisfactory quality. **2**

(b) Check their existing stock of sweatshirts, for labels/other information concerning how they wash. **2**

Study all earlier complaints to see if they can find a pattern (e.g. if a single supplier or item of equipment is involved); if so, contact/change supplier or remove the clothing/equipment. **2**

Survey their customers and check the responses they give. **2**

Discuss the situation with existing staff, e.g. to check motivation and ask opinions regarding the quality of the clothing/equipment. **2**

> **Examiner's tip** When thinking about this content, remember that there are two problem areas (clothing and equipment), so make comments on both of these.

(c) Provide induction training for all new employees; **1**
provide specialist sales training, e.g. with regard to customers' legal rights; **2**
provide higher levels of supervision for part-time staff; **1**
increase motivation, e.g. by financial or non-financial incentives. **2**

6 (a) Council focuses on providing services within budget limits; **2**
it may also run some operations (e.g. leisure centres) with a view to making a profit/surplus. **1**

Leisuretime is more concerned with profitability, market share and survival; **2**
it also wishes to give good customer service (otherwise sales are affected), as does the council. **1**

Question		Answer	Mark
(b)	**(i)**	No: it has achieved a 4.8% return (£12 000 as % of £250 000).	**2**
	(ii)	Profitability: profit is 5% of sales (£12 000 as % of £240 000).	**2**
		Liquidity: working capital ratio 1.5 : 1 (£30 000 current assets to £20 000 current liabilities).	**2**
(c)		Total profit is the same, even though sales have increased.	**1**
		This suggests that the Centre's sales mix might have changed, which is confirmed by the sales figures.	**1**
		The café sales are up by 80%, shop sales down to 60% of last year, aerobics also up by 80%, swimming pool sales remaining stable.	**2**
		This analysis suggests that the Centre should focus more on both its aerobics and café facilities;	**2**
		but it should also explore reasons why other sales are the same or falling.	**2**

Examiner's tip Expressing an increase or decrease as a percentage change (e.g. café sales up 80% rather than café sales up £8 000) is often an effective way of showing a trend.

7 (a)		8% of 150 000 is 12 000: expected population is therefore 162 000.	**2**
(b)	**(i)**	Large increase in under-10s, from 9% to 14% (increased by over half).	**2**
		11–20, 21–30, 31–40 age groups, numbers in each are expected to fall.	**2**
		Major increase in the over-50s (30% to 49% of population).	**2**
	(ii)	Increased under-10s: parents require child-care facilities when exercising, so Centre could consider offering crêche facilities;	**1**
		increased demand for swimming lessons for under-10s, so Centre needs to consider restructuring its swimming timetable;	**1**
		needs to consider whether it is employing sufficient trained staff;	**1**
		also consider hiring out the swimming pool and aerobics room for children's parties.	**1**
		11–40 age group: the most active users of the Centre facilities (especially the fitness and aerobics rooms), so Centre must try to maintain/increase sale of services to this age range;	**2**
		design leisure activities and offer additional sales promotions similar to 'Friday fun nights'.	**2**
		Over-50s: least physically active age group;	**1**
		they tend to concentrate on swimming rather than aerobics and fitness suite;	**1**
		Centre needs to offer additional swimming programmes;	**1**
		set up over-50s keep fit clubs.	**1**

Examiner's tip To answer this question well, you need to think carefully about how different age groups might use leisure and exercise facilities. By doing so, you can identify a number of important features which will help you look into the future and suggest sensible strategies for the Centre.

WORKING OUT YOUR RESULTS

As an experienced Chief and Principal Examiner, I would expect for each of the three key grades (A, C and F) the approximate marks for each question and in total to be as follows.

Grade A performance

Q1	Q2	Q3	Q4	Q5	Q6	Q7	Total
9	8	8	8	14	13	12	**72**

Grade C performance

Q1	Q2	Q3	Q4	Q5	Q6	Q7	Total
7	6	6	6	11	10	9	**55**

Grade F performance

Q1	Q2	Q3	Q4	Q5	Q6	Q7	Total
5	4	4	4	7	6	6	**36**